FACTS AT YOUR FINGERTIPS

INSECTS &
OTHER INVERTEBRATES

BROWN
BEAR
BOOKS

Published by Brown Bear Limited

An imprint of
The Brown Reference Group plc
68 Topstone Road
Redding
Connecticut
06896
USA
www.brownreference.com

ISBN-10: 1-933834-02-1
ISBN-13: 978-1-93383-402-3

Authors: Rod Preston-Mafham, Ken Preston-Mafham with Andrew Campbell and
        Amy-Jane Beer

Editorial Director: Lindsey Lowe

Project Director: Graham Bateman

Art Director: Steve McCurdy

Editor: Virginia Carter

Artists: Denys Ovenden, Richard Lewington with Simon Mendez

Printed in China

Jacket artwork: Front: Richard Lewington (Top Left, Center); Simon Mendez (Right).
        Reverse: Denys Ovenden.

Contents

Introduction

All life on Earth originated in the primeval seas some 4,000 million years ago. After eons of evolution a dizzying array of life has evolved. While the most obvious and most recently evolved (in relative terms) are the fish, amphibians, reptiles, birds, and mammals, there remains a wealth of other life forms that evolved long before these groups. Often small or invisible to the naked eye, the number of such species far surpasses that of the more obvious and familiar species. There are, for example, at least one million species of insects known, and the number is rising daily.

Facts at Your Fingertips: Insects & Other Invertebrates looks at the main groups of invertebrate life. Invertebrates are those animals that do not have a backbone: i.e. all animal life except fish, amphibians, reptiles, birds, and mammals.

Very little links the diverse forms and lifestyles of the groups covered here. Firstly, we look at four groups (phyla) of single-celled life, which form the kingdom Protista. Most are microscopic in size. Some have characteristics of true animals, some of plants, and some of both.

Our journey then takes us into the realm of true animals, kingdom Animalia. Kingdom Animalia contains 34 phyla, only one of which (Chordata) contains animals with backbones. Under the heading "Simple Animals" there are entries on a number of the more familiar invertebrate phyla (such as sponges and flatworms) or subgroups of phyla (such as jellyfish, sea anemones, and corals). In reality, none of these animals is truly simple. There is nothing simple about a

Rank	Scientific name	Common name
Kingdom	Animalia	Animals
Phylum	Arthropoda	Animals with an external skeleton and jointed limbs
Class	Insecta	Six-legged arthropods
Order	Lepidoptera	Butterflies and moths
Family	Danaidae	Milkweed butterflies
Genus	*Danaus*	
Species	*plexippus*	Monarch butterfly

The kingdom Animalia is subdivided into phyla, classes, orders, families, genera, and species. Above is the classification for the monarch butterfly.

sponge—a creature that is rooted to the spot and lacks even rudimentary organs yet is able to process thousands of liters of water a day in order to filter out food particles.

The largest proportion of entries in this book covers the phylum Arthropoda—the arthropods. They include the insects, millipedes, spiders, and crustaceans. The name "arthropod" is derived from the Greek, and literally means "jointed limb." However, the most important feature (and what sets them apart from other groups of animals) is the tough outer cuticle that forms the external skeleton. It covers all the internal organs as well as all the muscles that work the various external appendages. Arthropods molt the cuticle at various times to allow the body to grow.

The phylum Arthropoda is divided into a number of subphyla. Subphylum Crustacea (Crustaceans) have appendages, antennae, and limbs all made up of two branches. They are mainly aquatic creatures and include the crabs, lobsters, barnacles, prawns, and shrimps. All the remaining subphyla have unbranched appendages. Although they include aquatic species, the majority of them are terrestrial. Members of the subphylum Chelicerata (spiders and scorpions) have four pairs of legs, while the Myriapoda (centipedes and millipedes) all have more than five pairs of legs. The Hexapoda have just three pairs of legs and include the most successful group, the insects. In this book there are articles about many families of insects, arranged into their major groups such as beetles, true bugs, butterflies and moths, and wasps, ants, and bees.

The last stop on our journey through invertebrate life takes in two primarily aquatic phyla—the Mollusca (mollusks) and the Echinodermata (spiny-skinned animals). Mollusks usually have a shell of some sort and are either snail-, slug-, clam-, or squidlike in form. The exclusively marine echinoderms (starfish, sea urchins, and sea cucumbers) are either star-shaped or round and protected by a spiny skin.

Naming Animals

In order to discuss particular animals names are needed for the different kinds. For example, most people would regard the American monarch butterfly as one kind of butterfly and the cabbage white as another. All American monarchs look alike. They breed together and produce offspring the same as themselves. This popular distinction corresponds closely to the zoologist's definition of a species. All American monarchs belong to one species, and all cabbage whites to another.

Many animals have different names in different languages or more than one in a single language. Therefore, zoologists use an internationally recognized system for naming species, consisting of two-word names, usually in Latin or Greek. The American monarch butterfly is called *Danaus plexippus*, and the cabbage white is *Pieris rapae*.

The first word, for example, *Danaus,* is the genus (a group of similar species), which would include other monarchlike butterflies, such as the American queen. The second word, for example, *plexippus,* indicates the species in the genus, distinguishing it from the American queen, *Danaus gilippus*.

The same scientific names are recognized the world over. In this way the system allows precision and avoids confusion. However, it is possible for a species to have (or have had) two or more scientific names—it may have been described and named at different times without the zoologists realizing it was a single species. Usually when such a discrepancy is discovered, the first name takes priority.

As we have seen earlier, it is necessary to make statements about larger groups of animals. Classification makes this possible. In the example of the monarch butterfly all species that are similar to monarch butterflies are grouped in the family Danaidae, the milkweed butterflies; all butterfly and moth families are grouped in the order Lepidoptera; all

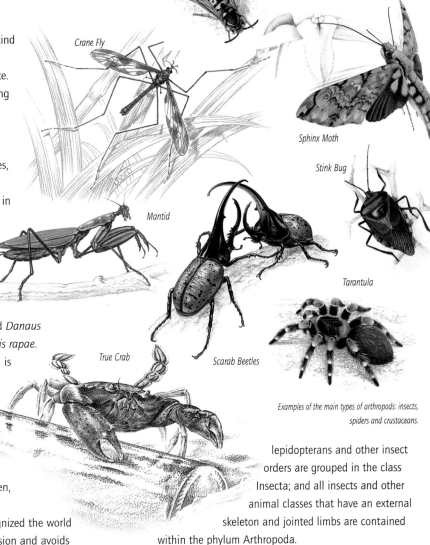

Examples of the main types of arthropods: insects, spiders and crustaceans.

lepidopterans and other insect orders are grouped in the class Insecta; and all insects and other animal classes that have an external skeleton and jointed limbs are contained within the phylum Arthropoda.

About this Book

In this book you will find illustrated entries on 112 groups of insects and other invertebrates. Each entry follows a fixed structure. The color-coded header strip denotes the category to which each animal belongs and gives its common name. There follows an illustration of a typical animal from the group, along with a caption specific to that animal. The fact panel then gives the scientific name of the animal in question and other taxonomic information. The sections that follow describe different features of the animals and their lifestyles.

Flagellates

Chlamydomonas is a plantlike flagellate that swims through water by beating a pair of hairlike flagella. Photosynthesis takes place in the horseshoe-shaped chloroplast. It is one of the commonest flagellates found in damp places throughout the world. Size microscopic up to 0.009 inches (0.024 mm) long.

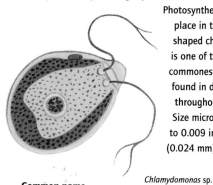

Chlamydomonas sp.

Common name
   Flagellates

Subphylum Mastigophora

Phylum Sarcomastigophora

Kingdom Protista

Number of species About 1,500

Size   Most are a few thousandths of an inch; some are just large enough to be seen with the naked eye

Key features Highly variable single-celled organisms; all have at least 1 long flagellum (organ of locomotion) at some stage in life cycle

Habits   Many live as commensals, parasites, or symbionts within other animals at some stage in life cycle

Breeding Highly varied and little understood; can be asexual or sexual with varying degrees of differentiation between male and female gametes (sex cells)

Diet   Plantlike flagellates produce at least some of their own food by photosynthesis; others feed by engulfing prey items or absorbing nutrients from a host

Habitat Mostly aquatic when not inside host

Distribution Worldwide

Amebas and Allies

One of the larger amebas, *Ameba proteus* is often observed in schools by students learning about simple animals. The species is aptly named—Proteus was a Greek god who could assume various forms. Size up to 0.2 inches (5 mm).

Ameba proteus

Common name Amebas, forams, heliozoans, radiolarians

Subphylum Sarcodina

Phylum Sarcomastigophora

Kingdom Protista

Number of species About 11,500

Size   Mostly microscopic, but some amebas reach 0.2 in (5 mm), and some forams grow to 1 in (2.5 cm) or more; radiolarians may form colonies 8 in (20 cm) long

Key features Asymmetrical or spherical protists lacking flagellae, but with variable pseudopods; may be naked or secrete a proteinaceous or siliceous shell, test, or skeleton

Habits   Aquatic, free living, occasionally parasitic

Breeding Sexual by conjugation or asexual by fission or schizogony

Diet   Feed by engulfing other organisms, mainly bacteria and organic matter

Habitat Wherever there is moisture; in oceans, rivers, lakes, puddles, soil, caves, and in and around multicellular plants and animals; several species have been collected from the earth's upper atmosphere

Distribution Worldwide

Ciliates

Paramecium is surrounded by a tough coating with numerous cilia. It also has a distinct furrow leading to the cytostome, or cell mouth.

Length about 0.02 inches (0.5 mm).

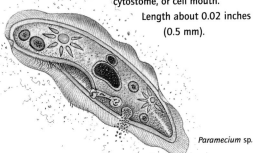

Paramecium sp.

Common name Ciliates

Phylum Ciliophora

Kingdom Protista

Number of species About 8,000 known, with many more yet to be described

Size Generally microscopic, from a few microns to 0.1 in (3 mm) in length

Key features Single-celled organisms with two distinct types of nuclei and external cilia; internal structure may be very complex

Habits Mostly free living; occasionally parasitic; many have resistant cyst phase

Breeding Mostly asexual by binary fission; no males or females—sexual reproduction involves conjugation of compatible cell types

Diet Mostly bacteria that are engulfed and digested in cell vacuoles

Habitat Mainly fresh water

Distribution Worldwide

Malaria

Four *Plasmodium* species are responsible for causing malaria in humans. The disease has been eradicated in the United States, but in the developing world control measures have had little effect to date.

Plasmodium sp.

Common name Malaria

Phylum Apicomplexa (formerly Sporozoa)

Kingdom Protista

Number of species About 4,000 described to date

Size Mostly a few microns, occasionally up to 0.4 in (10 mm) long

Key features Single cells, usually elongate; tips of the cell contain a complex of filaments

Habits Parasitic

Breeding Life cycles often involve sexual and asexual phases and multiple hosts

Diet Nutrients absorbed from host

Habitat Bodies of other animals, either inside or alongside host cells

Distribution Worldwide, especially prevalent in tropical regions

Sponges

Columns of the brown tube sponge, *Agelas conifera*, rise from the seabed like smokestacks. This sponge is found in seas around the Bahamas, the Caribbean, and Florida. Growing up to 36 inches (90 cm) tall, brown tube sponges are sometimes home to small fish that live inside their hollow core.

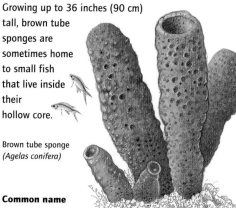

Brown tube sponge
(*Agelas conifera*)

Common name
 Sponges

Phylum Porifera

Number of species About 5,000

Size Variable, from 0.1 in (2.5 mm) to 40 in (100 cm) or more in height; occasionally over 10 ft (3 m) across

Key features Simple, radially symmetrical but irregularly shaped animals; made up of largely undifferentiated (nonspecialized) tissues around a system of channels and chambers through which water can flow; mostly colorful, in shades of red, orange, purple, yellow, and green; occasionally dull and inconspicuous

Habits Nonmoving, usually attached to hard substratum

Breeding Asexual by budding or production of gemmules (cell packets), or sexual with internal fertilization and direct development into small adults

Diet Small bacteria, protists, and particles of organic material

Habitat Mostly marine at all depths; some freshwater species exist

Distribution Worldwide

Hydrozoans

Obelia geniculata is a distinctive species, with slender zigzag stems. It forms colonies of polyps and is common in shallow, rocky habitats of northwestern Europe, although it is almost worldwide in its distribution. Colonies can grow up to 1.6 inches (4 cm) in height.

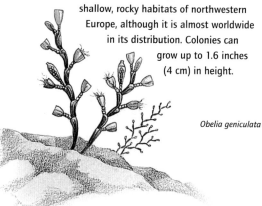

Obelia geniculata

Common name Hydrozoans, hydroids, hydrocorals, hydras, Portuguese men-of-war

Class Hydrozoa

Phylum Cnidaria

Number of species About 3,000

Size Varies greatly; individual polyps mostly very small, but hydroid colonies can be up to 6 in (15 cm) tall; some deep-sea species produce solitary polyps over 6 ft (1.8 m) long; floating Portuguese man-of-war colonies can be several feet long including tentacles

Key features Very varied group; in all cases mesoglea lacks cells; stinging cells are on the outside of the body, never inside; gonads shed gametes externally; basic forms include solitary and colonial polyps with or without a hard skeleton and some small medusae

Habits Live in open seas, attached directly to substratum

Breeding Asexual by budding (may lead to separate individuals or expansion into a colony); sexual reproduction occurs in medusa phase or in gonophores (reproductive zooids) attached to polyp colony

Diet Small particles of food collected from the water; prey animals killed by stinging cnidocytes

Habitat Aquatic, mostly marine; some species (notably hydras) live in fresh water

Distribution Worldwide

Jellyfish

The adult medusa of the moon jellyfish, *Aurelia aurita*. The moon jellyfish has global distribution and can survive a wide range of sea temperatures. Its sting causes an itchy rash. Diameter 10 inches (25 cm).

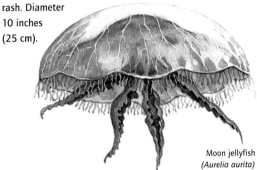

Moon jellyfish
(*Aurelia aurita*)

Common name Jellyfish (sea jellies)

Class Scyphozoa and Cubozoa

Phylum Cnidaria

Number of species About 200

Size Mature medusae measure 0.5 in (13 mm) to 6.5 ft (2 m) in diameter

Key features In most species the predominant form is a saucer-, bell-, or helmet-shaped medusa with fringe of tentacles around the edge or elaborate arms trailing from mouth in center of underside

Habits Most swim freely in open seas by means of pulsating bell; may migrate vertically to feed in shallower water at night

Breeding Medusae shed gametes via mouth; fertilization takes place in the water; embryos develop via 2 larval stages: The swimming planula larva develops into fixed polyplike scyphistoma larva, from which miniature medusae are produced asexually

Diet A wide variety of invertebrate prey and some fish killed by stinging cells on tentacles or oral arms

Habitat Marine, mostly open seas, occasionally bottom dwellers

Distribution Worldwide

Sea Anemones

Metridium senile, the frilled anemone, is found from the Arctic to southern California. Large specimens can have 1,000 tentacles. Height up to 18 inches (46 cm). *Actinia equina*, the beadlet anemone, is from the Atlantic and Mediterranean. It is the most common anemone found on northern European rocky shores. Height about 3 inches (7 cm).

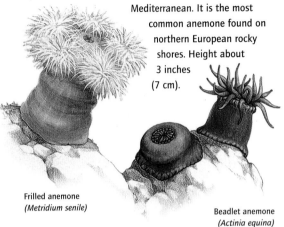

Frilled anemone
(*Metridium senile*)

Beadlet anemone
(*Actinia equina*)

Common name Sea anemones

Order Actinaria

Class Anthozoa (part)

Phylum Cnidaria

Number of species About 1,000

Size Up to 40 in (100 cm) in diameter

Key features Solitary polyps with predominantly 6-fold symmetry; often very colorful

Habits Mostly slow moving with long periods attached to a single spot; may creep, climb, burrow, or swim; solitary

Breeding Sexual reproduction results in planula larva that settles and metamorphoses into miniature polyp; most species also reproduce asexually by binary fission or regeneration from small fragments of tissue

Diet Various invertebrate prey; occasionally snare fish with stinging tentacles; many species receive proportion of nutritional requirements from symbiotic algae

Habitat Marine, from coastal zones to deep oceans

Distribution In all oceans and adjoining seas worldwide

Corals

Colonies of the soft coral *Alcyonium digitatum*, or dead man's fingers, can be found around the coasts of Western Europe. Colonies can grow up to 8 inches (20 cm) in height.

Dead man's fingers
(Alcyonium digitatum)

Common name
    Stony corals,
    soft corals, horny corals,
    sea pens, sea fans

Class   Anthozoa (part)

Phylum Cnidaria

Number of species About 5,000

Size   Solitary forms up to 20 in (50 cm) in diameter; polyps of colonial forms usually less than 0.2 in (5 mm) in diameter; colonies up to several feet across; entire reefs can extend for miles

Key features Mostly colonial polyps, either soft bodied or overlying a stony skeleton of secreted calcium carbonate; colony may be encrusting or erect, making antler, feather, fan, plate, slipper, or boulder shape; colors include vibrant shades of red, purple, orange, green, and blue or brown and black

Habits Sessile (attached by the substratum); colonial, but compete aggressively for growing space

Breeding Colonies grow by asexual budding; sexual reproduction involves simultaneous shedding of gametes into the water; fertilization leads to development of free-swimming planula larvae that disperse and settle to found new colonies elsewhere

Diet   Reef-building (hermatypic) corals gain most of their nutrients from symbiotic algae living inside each polyp; other food, mainly plankton and bacteria, is captured from water by tentacles

Habitat Marine, mostly shallow tropical seas; some specialized corals live in deeper and colder water

Distribution Worldwide, mainly in the tropics

Flatworms and Tapeworms

Gliding over rocks and seaweed in shallow seas, the free-swimming candystripe flatworm, *Prostheceraeus vittatus*, is occasionally seen by divers. It lives beneath stones in muddy habitats in the Atlantic Ocean and the North Sea. Length 2 inches (5 cm).

Candystripe flatworm
(Prostheceraeus vittatus)

Common name Flatworms, tapeworms, flukes

Phylum Platyhelminthes

Number of species About 25,000

Size   From about 0.001 in (0.03 mm) to 13 ft (4 m); occasionally reach 65 ft (20 m)

Key features Flattened body with front and rear end; no coelom (body cavity), gut often absent or incomplete, or may be finely branched, but with no anus; anterior end may carry simple sense organs such as light-sensitive ocelli

Habits Free living and parasitic, often with several hosts; move by swimming or crawling

Breeding Sexual and asexual, most species hermaphrodite, but some dioecious (having either male or female sexual organs); development may be direct from egg to adult or involve metamorphosis from a free-living larval form; life cycle may involve more than 1 host

Diet   Free-living species may be carnivorous or scavenging; parasites feed on body fluids or gut contents of host

Habitat Free-living species are mostly aquatic; some have evolved to live in humid places on land; parasitic species are carried with hosts

Distribution Worldwide

Beard Worms

Oligobrachia ivanovi is a beard worm species from the northeastern Atlantic. It is shown partly exposed from its tube. Beard worms are found mainly at great depths. Length over 36 inches (1 m).

Oligobrachia ivanovi

Common name Beard worms

Phylum Pogonophora

Number of species About 150

Size Most 2 in (5 cm) to 30 in (80 cm) long, some giants grow to about 6.5 ft (1.9 m)

Key features Segmented body largely encased in long chitinous tube; front section bears "beard" of fine tentacles; mouth and gut are absent in adult form

Habits Sessile; tube dwelling

Reproduction Sperm released into the water by males finds its way into the tubes of females; trochophore larvae develop from eggs fertilized inside the tube, then swim free for a short time before settling somewhere close by to begin adult life

Diet Some organic molecules absorbed from the water, most food is supplied by bacteria living within the animal that produce carbohydrates by the process of chemosynthesis

Habitat Deep ocean, from 330 ft (100 m) to the deepest trenches

Distribution Not fully known, but examples are known from all oceans

Ragworms and Allies

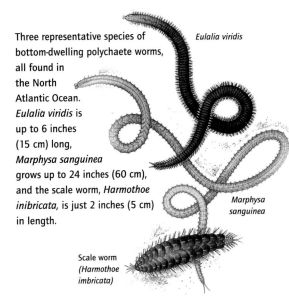

Three representative species of bottom-dwelling polychaete worms, all found in the North Atlantic Ocean. *Eulalia viridis* is up to 6 inches (15 cm) long, *Marphysa sanguinea* grows up to 24 inches (60 cm), and the scale worm, *Harmothoe inibricata*, is just 2 inches (5 cm) in length.

Eulalia viridis

Marphysa sanguinea

Scale worm (*Harmothoe imbricata*)

Common name Ragworms, lugworms, fan worms, and many others

Class Polychaeta

Phylum Annelida

Number of species Almost 10,000

Size 0.04 in (1 mm) to 9.8 ft (3 m) long

Key features Long, slightly flattened body made up of many segments bearing diverse paired, bristly appendages called parapodia; several species bear crown of feeding tentacles; many species are very colorful

Habits Crawling, free-swimming, burrowing, or sedentary tube dwellers; some commensal and parasitic forms are known

Reproduction Mostly sexual; males and females release gametes into the water for external fertilization; mass spawning may be carried out by specialized reproductive individuals called epitokes; ciliated trochophore larvae undergo gradual metamorphosis before attaining adult form

Diet Very varied; may be carnivores, herbivores, or detritus feeders; food is obtained by active hunting, grazing, nonselective deposit feeding, or filter feeding

Habitat Mostly marine and bottom dwelling from tidal zone to deep ocean

Distribution Worldwide

Earthworms

Leeches

The European common earthworm, *Lumbricus terrestris*, is found wherever there is moisture, including grass, mud, and beneath stones. Length 3.5-12 inches (9-30 cm).

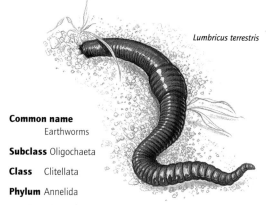

Lumbricus terrestris

Common name
Earthworms

Subclass Oligochaeta

Class Clitellata

Phylum Annelida

Number of species About 3,100

Size From 1 in (2.5 cm) to 13 ft (4 m) long

Key features Long, soft, moist body with annular rings representing body segments; mostly reddish in color, with a few short, stiff hairs sprouting from each segment; in sexually mature adults several segments swell to form the saddle, or clitellum

Habits Mostly soil dwelling or aquatic; use hydraulic action to burrow and swim

Reproduction Asexual by splitting in two (fission) in many aquatic species; sexual reproduction involves mating of hermaphrodite pairs; fertilized eggs are shed into cocoon formed by the clitellum

Diet Mostly plant material

Habitat Soil; fresh water

Distribution Worldwide except Antarctica and arid deserts

The medicinal leech, *Hirudo medicinalis*, is the famous blood-letting leech used by doctors over the centuries to relieve patients of all manner of symptoms. Its use was so widespread that the leech almost became extinct in Britain in the 19th century. It is shown above feeding on a three-spined stickleback. Length up to 6 inches (15 cm).

Medicinal leech *(Hirudo medicinalis)*

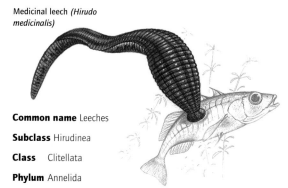

Common name Leeches

Subclass Hirudinea

Class Clitellata

Phylum Annelida

Number of species About 500

Size 0.4 in (10 mm) to 19 in (50 cm)

Key features Elongated and flattened, with suckers at front and rear ends; body may be bloated after feeding; body lacks externally obvious segmentation and segmental appendages; color variable, often some shade of black, brown, or green

Habits Free living; parasitic on exterior of host; move by "looping" like caterpillars or swim with muscular wavelike contractions of body

Breeding Protandrous hermaphrodites (change sex from male to female); mating occurs; fertilization of eggs is internal following insemination, embryos develop in cocoon secreted by the clitellum; eggs hatch into miniature adults—no larval stage

Diet Mostly parasitic bloodsuckers; a few species are carnivorous

Habitat Most leeches live in fresh water, but there are some specialized marine forms and a number of species that are able to live on land

Distribution All continents except Antarctica, most common in warm tropical lakes and rivers and on almost all landmasses

Katydids

Ommatopia pictifolia from Brazil closely resembles a dead leaf. Body length 1 inch (2.5 cm).

Ommatopia pictifolia

Common name Katydids (long-horned grasshoppers) (U.S.), bush crickets (U.K.)

Family Tettigoniidae

Suborder Ensifera

Order Orthoptera

Class/Subphylum Insecta/Hexapoda

Number of species About 5,000 (about 250 U.S.)

Size From about 0.4 in (10 mm) to 5 in (13 cm)

Key features Body form anything from long and slim to short and fat, sometimes with ornamentations on the head and thorax; jumping hind legs tend to be long and slender; forewings (the tegmina) often look like leaves, living or dead; some species lack wings altogether; antennae long and slim, sometimes more than twice the body length; female ovipositor curved and flattened from side to side

Habits Mainly active during the hours of darkness but often seen during the day when they jump into the air and take flight if disturbed; some can be found feeding on flowers during the day

Breeding Males usually attract females by singing; mating takes place at night and is therefore not often seen; females use ovipositors to insert their eggs into plants or the ground

Diet Most feed on plant material, while many will also eat other insects if they can catch them; some katydids are completely predaceous, only feeding on other arthropods

Habitat Among vegetation in meadows, parks, gardens, broad-leaved forests, mountains, deserts, and marshes

Distribution Widespread around the world, with the greatest variety of species in the tropics

Crickets

The black cricket, *Gryllus bimaculatus*, is native to southern Europe. It is bred commercially as lizard food. Being large and stocky it cannot fly, and the male sings a birdlike song day and night. Body length 1–1.2 inches (2.5–3.0 cm).

Black cricket
(Gryllus bimaculatus)

Common name Crickets

Family Gryllidae

Suborder Ensifera

Order Orthoptera

Class/Subphylum Insecta/Hexapoda

Number of species About 2,000 (about 100 U.S.)

Size From about 0.06 in (1.5 mm) to 2.3 in (6 cm)

Key features Separated from related insects, such as katydids, by the fact that crickets have only 3 segments in the tarsus of the middle leg, while katydids have 4; jumping hind legs short and fairly stout; antennae long and slim, sometimes more than twice the body length; female ovipositor straight and cylindrical; hearing organ on each front leg

Habits During the day generally found on the ground, sheltering under stones and logs or among vegetation; most are active at night, but some are day active; some males dig burrows

Breeding Males usually attract females by "singing"; mating takes place at night and therefore not often seen; females use ovipositor to insert eggs in the ground, into crevices, and sometimes into plants; females lay just 1 egg at a time

Diet Perhaps the most omnivorous of the Orthoptera, feeding on both plants and other insects; flowers—especially the pollen-rich anthers—a favorite of some species

Habitat Meadows, parks, gardens, forests, mountains, deserts, and caves; also ants' nests

Distribution Widespread around the world

Crane Flies

The European species, *Tipula maxima,* is one of the largest crane flies, with wings conspicuously marked with patches of brown. It is a particular favorite of the trout, which will often come to the surface of the pond or lake to feed on these crane flies when they settle on the water in sufficient numbers. Body length up to 1.2 inches (3 cm).

Tipula maxima

Common name
  Crane flies (daddy-longlegs)

Family Tipulidae

Suborder Nematocera

Order   Diptera

Class/Subphylum Insecta/Hexapoda

Number of species About 14,000 (about 1,600 U.S.)

Size   From about 0.3 in (8 mm) to 2 in (5 cm)

Key features Body usually long and slim; long legs; wings may be clear or with smoky patterns; ocelli not present; face often drawn out into a definite snout; larva somewhat caterpillarlike with a definite head

Habits Adults usually sit in the shade during the day, feeding occasionally at suitable flowers; many have the habit of "bobbing" the body up and down when disturbed; larvae live in the soil, in water, or in dead wood

Breeding Males may search actively for females or they may come together in mating swarms; eggs laid in the soil or in water; larvae aquatic or terrestrial

Diet   Adults take water and nectar; larvae feed on plants, algae, dead wood, worms, and larvae of other insects

Habitat Forests, meadows, sides of streams and lakes, gardens, mountains, and the coast

Distribution Widespread around the world, especially humid tropical areas

---

Mosquitoes and Gnats

The ring-legged mosquito, *Culiseta annulata,* can be easily identified by the black-and-white bands on its legs. It is one of the largest mosquitoes, whose bite can be painful, although it probably does not carry any diseases. It is found all over Europe. Body length 0.2 inches (5 mm).

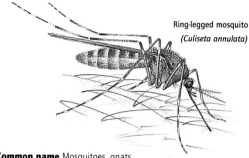

Ring-legged mosquito
(Culiseta annulata)

Common name Mosquitoes, gnats

Family Culicidae

Suborder Nematocera

Order   Diptera

Class/Subphylum Insecta/Hexapoda

Number of species About 3,000 (over 150 U.S.)

Size   From about 0.2 in (5 mm) to around 0.3 in (8 mm)

Key features Slender body, long legs, and rigid, piercing mouthparts (except in the gnats); ocelli not present; males of most species have featherlike antennae

Habits May be diurnal or nocturnal; tend to rest in the shade; blood feeders attracted to host animals by the carbon dioxide they breathe out

Breeding Females whine to attract males; often form mating swarms; females lay their eggs on the surface of water

Diet   Male mosquitoes feed on nectar and fruit juices; females feed similarly, but a number are also blood feeders; larvae are aquatic filter feeders or nibble at underwater plant remains and algae; a few feed on other mosquito larvae

Habitat Usually found near water in which they can breed; also forests with plenty of water-filled holes in trees; lake- and pond-side vegetation, marshes, estuaries, human habitations, outhouses, stables, and so on

Distribution Worldwide even into the Arctic

Horseflies and Deerflies

The 3-spot horsefly, *Tabanus trimaculatus*, is found in the United States and feeds on deer, moose, and domestic livestock. It can also attack humans. Body length 0.5–0.6 inches (13-15 mm). The "blinder" deerfly, *Chrysops caecutiens*, is from Europe. It is called the "blinder" because it bites its host's eyelids, causing them to swell up and reduce the animal's ability to see. Body length 0.5–0.6 inches (13–15 mm).

3-spot horsefly *(Tabanus trimaculatus)*   "Blinder"deerfly *(Chrysops caecutiens)*

Common name Horseflies, deerflies (elephant flies, clegs)

Family Tabanidae

Suborder Brachycera

Order Diptera

Class/Subphylum Insecta/Hexapoda

Number of species Around 3,000 (350 U.S.)

Size From 0.2 in (5 mm) to 1 in (2.5 cm)

Key features Eyes large, usually with brightly colored patterns; body stout; wings often with darker patterning; biting proboscis; eyes of male nearly touching on top of head

Habits Tend to be active on sunny days; usually avoid shade when biting; stealthy flight when approaching hosts to feed

Breeding Males either form individual territories and mate with passing females or gather in swarms

Diet Males feed only at flowers; females take nectar and blood; larvae mainly predaceous, while others feed on decaying vegetable matter

Habitat Wherever the mammals they feed on are found; larvae in water or damp soil

Distribution Worldwide—tropics, temperate zones, and the Arctic

Robber Flies

A robber fly, *Machimus atricapillus*, seizes a lacewing in flight. This species is found in Europe. Body length 0.4 inches (10 mm).

Machimus atricapillus

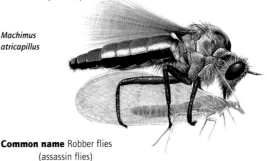

Common name Robber flies (assassin flies)

Family Asilidae

Suborder Brachycera

Order Diptera

Class/Subphylum Insecta/Hexapoda

Number of species About 6,500 (983 U.S.)

Size From about 0.3 in (8 mm) to 1.2 in (3 cm)

Key features Eyes very large in relation to the head, bulging both upward and forward; ocelli present; all of the body, but especially the head, heavily bristled; powerful proboscis; hind legs powerful, used for grasping prey

Habits Adult flies like bright sunshine; sit around on vegetation, rocks, or on the ground waiting for passing insects; mostly strong fliers that catch other insects, especially other flies, in midair; a number of species are good mimics of bees and wasps

Breeding Some species have elaborate courtship rituals; eggs laid on or in the soil, plants, or rotting wood

Diet Adults highly predaceous, sucking the insides out of their insect prey; larvae feed on vegetable matter in soil; some may be carnivorous

Habitat Forests, savanna, grassland, deserts, mountains, and sand dunes

Distribution Worldwide

Hover Flies

Hover flies are common visitors to garden flowers. Many people mistake some of the commonest species for bees. *Milesia crabroniformis* is found in southern Europe and the Mediterranean region. Body length 0.9–1 inches (23–27 mm). The drone fly, *Eristalis tenax*, is an important pollinator, with worldwide distribution. Body length 0.5–0.6 inches (12–15 mm).

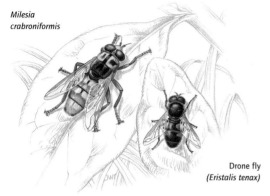

Milesia crabroniformis

Drone fly
(Eristalis tenax)

Common name Hover flies (flower flies)

Family Syrphidae

Suborder Brachycera

Order Diptera

Class/Subphylum Insecta/Hexapoda

Number of species About 6,000 (around 950 U.S.)

Size From about 0.2 in (5 mm) to 1 in (2.5 cm)

Key features Body often striped, mimicking bees or wasps; mouthparts adapted for sucking up nectar; eyes quite large

Habits Sun loving; visit flowers; often form large swarms; usually spend much of their time in hovering flight, sometimes for no obvious reason

Breeding Hovering males attract females, or males may seek out females on foliage and hover over them; eggs laid in various places depending on food requirements of larvae

Diet Adults are nectar feeders; some species also feed on pollen; larvae carnivorous or feed on vegetable matter

Habitat Almost anywhere with flowers from which they can feed

Distribution Worldwide, including the tropics, but at their greatest numbers in temperate zones

Small Fruit Flies

The fruit fly *Drosophila melanogaster* is found worldwide. It is also the fly species that is probably best known to scientists, who have used it in genetic research for almost a century. Body length about 0.1 inches (3–4 mm).

Drosophila melanogaster

Common name Small fruit flies (vinegar flies, pomace flies)

Family Drosophilidae

Suborder Brachycera

Order Diptera

Class/Subphylum Insecta/Hexapoda

Number of species 2,800 (117 U.S.)

Size From 0.08 in (2 mm) to around 0.3 in (8 mm)

Key features Small, rather plump flies; eyes often red; wings may be patterned; males may have modifications of parts of the body relating to courtship

Habits Adults most likely to be found on decaying fruit or fermenting sap flows on damaged plants

Breeding Courtship often quite complex, with males "singing" to females

Diet Adults take juices from rotting fruit or sap flows; larvae feed on fermentation products, or mine leaves; may be carnivorous or parasitic

Habitat Woodland, rain forest, indoors (especially in breweries, wineries, and canteens); also found on garbage heaps

Distribution Worldwide but more common in warmer parts

Bot and Warble Flies

The common warble fly, *Hypoderma bovis*, is found in the Northern Hemisphere between March and the end of May. It lays its eggs on cattle, which recognize the sound of the fly approaching and attempt evasive action, known as "gadding." These disturbances in feeding can result in decreased yield of milk or meat from the cattle. Body length 0.4-0.6 inches (10-14 mm).

Common warble fly
(*Hypoderma bovis*)

Common name Bot flies (nostril flies), warble flies

Family Oestridae

Suborder Brachycera

Order Diptera

Class/Subphylum Insecta/Hexapoda

Number of species 65 (41 U.S.)

Size From 0.4 in (10 mm) to 1 in (2.5 cm)

Key features Adults heavily built and rather plump; may resemble bees

Habits Adult flies are generally short-lived and stay close to the host animal on which their larvae will feed

Breeding Males of some species defend territories; females lay eggs or deposit live larvae on host; some species use other insects to carry eggs to host

Diet Adults not known to feed; larvae are internal parasites of vertebrates, including humans

Habitat Adults seldom seen; larvae of some species may be seen under the skin of the host

Distribution Worldwide, with a number of species having been spread by humans

Dung Flies

The common yellow dung fly, *Scathophaga stercoraria*, is found worldwide. It was brought to the New World by the first European colonists on their livestock. Body length 0.3-0.4 inches (8-10 mm).

Scathophaga stercoraria

Common name Dung flies

Family Scathophagidae

Suborder Brachycera

Order Diptera

Class/Subphylum Insecta/Hexapoda

Number of species 500 (about 150 U.S.)

Size From 0.2 in (5 mm) to 0.4 in (10 mm)

Key features Rounded head bearing (in predatory species) a well-developed proboscis with "teeth" at the end; often with a rather "furry" body

Habits Dung feeders assemble on or near sources of dung, although adults also visit flowers

Breeding Males known to form groups waiting for females to arrive or to seek out females on vegetation in other species

Diet In some species adults feed on other flies; larvae may be dung or plant feeders (including leaf mining), or predators

Habitat Wherever there are dung-producing animals; otherwise where food plants occur and even the seashore

Distribution North America, Europe, and nontropical Asia, with just a few species in Africa and South America; *Scathophaga stercoraria* found worldwide on cattle dung

Houseflies and Relatives

Musca domestica, the common housefly, breeds in manure, garbage, and rotting vegetable matter. It is found all over the world and can spread diseases and cause food poisoning due to its habit of feeding on both excrement and human food. Body length 0.2–0.3 inches (5–7 mm).

Common housefly (*Musca domestica*)

Common name Houseflies, face flies, stable flies, horn flies

Family Muscidae

Suborder Brachycera

Order Diptera

Class/Subphylum Insecta/Hexapoda

Number of species 4,000 (622 U.S.)

Size From 0.1 in (3 mm) to 0.5 in (13 mm)

Key features Mostly small; differ from other families in lack of certain bristles on thorax; common housefly is a typical muscid

Habits Typically sit around on vegetation or in houses, stables, and other buildings

Breeding Some species court in flight; female lays eggs on or near food

Diet Adults feed on blood, sweat, and plant and fruit juices; larvae feed on decaying plants, dung, and dead animals; can be predators

Habitat Outside in all types of habitat in all types of climate; human habitations, trash heaps, cowsheds, and stables

Distribution Worldwide—many common species have been spread by humans

Blow Flies

Calliphora vomitoria is a very common blow fly, often seen inside houses. Females are known to lay eggs in open wounds, where the larvae grow and feed. On live animals such an infestation is known as myiasis. Body length 0.5 inches (13 mm).

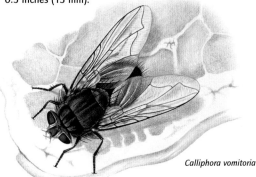

Calliphora vomitoria

Common name Blow flies (bluebottle flies, greenbottle flies)

Family Calliphoridae

Suborder Brachycera

Order Diptera

Class/Subphylum Insecta/Hexapoda

Number of species 1,000 (78 U.S.)

Size From 0.3 in (8 mm) to 0.6 in (15 mm)

Key features Usually shiny, blue, black, or green flies; separated from other fly families by arrangement of bristles on thorax

Habits Often seen on dead and decaying animals where females lay eggs

Breeding Females seek out laying sites by smell and lay large numbers of eggs

Diet Adults take liquid foods such as fruit juices; larvae feed on decaying animals, suck blood, or are parasitic

Habitat Deserts, grasslands, temperate and tropical forests, seashore, human habitations, food-processing plants, and trash heaps

Distribution All regions of the world

Water Striders

The common water strider, *Gerris lacustris*, can be found on almost any stretch of still, fresh water. The bugs use their hind two pairs of legs to move across the water, leaving the short front legs free to catch food. Length 0.3 inches (8 mm).

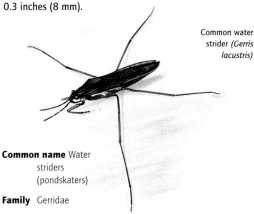

Common water strider *(Gerris lacustris)*

Common name Water striders (pondskaters)

Family Gerridae

Suborder Heteroptera

Order Hemiptera

Class/Subphylum Insecta/Hexapoda

Number of species About 500 (45 U.S.)

Size From about 0.2 in (5 mm) to 0.7 in (18 mm)

Key features Male usually smaller than female; middle and hind legs much longer than body and splayed out sideways for skating on water; middle legs closer to hind legs than to front legs; front legs adapted for grasping prey; body oval to elongate, covered in dense layer of "hairs" that prevent it from becoming wet; wings may be full, partial, or absent; eyes large

Habits Skating around on the surface of water in search of prey

Breeding Once he has found a mate, the male usually stays on the female's back; eggs laid on floating plants or among debris

Diet Small insects that have fallen on the water, small fish, tadpoles; some cannibalism of nymphs is recorded; prey often shared

Habitat All types of freshwater habitat such as ponds, lakes, streams, rivers, canals, and animal water troughs, but excluding very fast-moving water; also the surface of the sea

Distribution Worldwide for freshwater species; some *Halobates* species are oceanic

Water Scorpions

The water stick insect, *Ranatra linearis*, hangs from the surface by its breathing siphon and waits to catch prey such as water fleas with its front legs. It is not a good swimmer and mostly crawls among the weeds. Length (without siphon) 1 inch (2.5 cm).

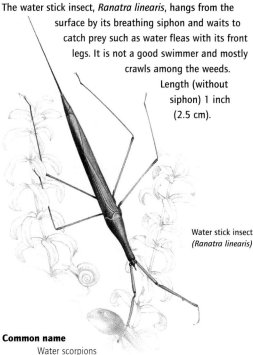

Water stick insect *(Ranatra linearis)*

Common name Water scorpions (water stick insects)

Family Nepidae

Suborder Heteroptera

Order Hemiptera

Class/Subphylum Insecta/Hexapoda

Number of species About 200 (13 U.S.)

Size From about 0.7 in (18 mm) to 2 in (5 cm)

Key features Front legs adapted for grasping prey; body flattened and oval or long and sticklike; fully winged and capable of flight; a long, thin breathing tube extends from the hind end

Habits Walk around on vegetation beneath the water hunting for prey; may hang below surface with breathing tube just above surface, taking in air

Breeding Eggs laid inside aquatic plants; males of some species use their front legs to grasp the female during mating

Diet Insect larvae, tadpoles, and small crustaceans such as water fleas

Habitat Still and slow-moving water of ponds, lakes, canals, and rivers

Distribution Worldwide in suitable habitats, especially in tropical regions

Backswimmers

The common backswimmer, *Notonecta glauca*, is widespread throughout Europe and lives in ponds, ditches, and canals. It swims upside down, propelled by two long legs that paddle like oars, making it look like a rowboat. Length up to 0.8 inches (20 mm).

Common
backswimmer
(Notonecta glauca)

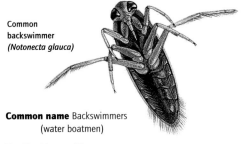

Common name Backswimmers
(water boatmen)

Family Notonectidae

Suborder Heteroptera

Order Hemiptera

Class/Subphylum Insecta/Hexapoda

Number of species About 300 (35 U.S.)

Size From about 0.2 in (5 mm) to 0.6 in (15 mm)

Key features Body boat shaped, flat on the underside; usually hang head down from water surface, showing underside; eyes large; ears present in both sexes; rostrum strong and sharp; front legs used to grasp prey; hind legs long, fringed with hairs and used as paddles; wings well developed; underside of abdomen bears water-repellent hairs

Habits All species are strong swimmers, coming to the surface regularly to replenish air supply; also strong fliers, moving from one area of water to another

Breeding In some species males stridulate to attract females; eggs attached to objects in the water, such as stones or plants

Diet Aquatic animals including insect larvae, tadpoles, and small fish as well as insects that have fallen into the water

Habitat Lakes and ponds, water tanks, and animal water troughs

Distribution Worldwide

Plant Bugs

Lygus rugulipennis is a pest of greenhouse cucumber crops. Length approximately 0.2 inches (5–6 mm). *Deraeocoris ruber* feeds on the developing fruit and seeds of numerous plants, as well as on aphids and other small insects. Length 0.2–0.3 inches (6–8 mm). Both species are widespread in the Northern Hemisphere.

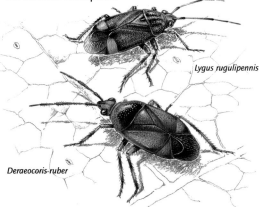

Lygus rugulipennis

Deraeocoris ruber

Common name Plant bugs (leaf bugs, capsid bugs)

Family Miridae

Suborder Heteroptera

Order Hemiptera

Class/Subphylum Insecta/Hexapoda

Number of species About 10,000 (about 1,800 U.S.)

Size From about 0.12 in (3 mm) to 0.6 in (15 mm)

Key features Shape variable; some long and thin, others short, broad, and rather soft bodied; usually fully winged but may have short wings or lack them altogether; often brightly colored, but many species also have cryptic coloration, usually rather shiny; separated from other bug families by having a 4-segmented rostrum, 4-segmented antennae, and by absence of ocelli

Habits Most often found running around on the plant species with which they are associated

Breeding Females insert eggs into the tissues of their food plants or beneath bark

Diet Many species feed on plants and include pests of crops; others are predaceous, feeding on small insects; some species rob spiders' webs

Habitat Found from the ground up to the tops of the highest trees in almost any habitat where suitable plants grow

Distribution Worldwide

Bedbugs

The human bedbug, *Cimex lectularius*, is a notorious worldwide pest. It feeds not only on humans but also on bats, chickens, and other domestic animals. When feeding, it moves slowly over the skin, biting every few steps. It can survive for over a year without a blood meal. Length 0.2–0.3 inches (4–7 mm).

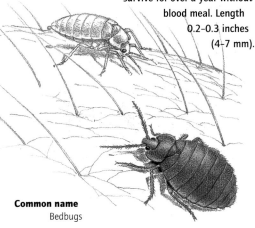

Human bedbug
(Cimex lectularius)

Common name
　Bedbugs

Family Cimicidae

Suborder Heteroptera

Order Hemiptera

Class/Subphylum Insecta/Hexapoda

Number of species About 80 (4 U.S.)

Size From about 0.1 in (3 mm) to 0.2 in (5 mm)

Key features Body oval and flattened (appearing more rounded after a blood feed); color yellowish to brown; wingless

Habits All species are parasites on surface of birds and mammals, including humans; active by night, when they come out to feed

Breeding Male bugs penetrate the body of the female and inject sperm into the body fluid; eggs are laid in crevices near the host animal

Diet Blood feeders

Habitat Birds' nests, cellars, and caves inhabited by bats; human habitations

Distribution Worldwide, but mostly in the tropics

Assassin Bugs

An *Acanthaspis* sp. assassin bug feeds on a caterpillar. *Acanthaspis* sp. have been found in West Africa, where they prey on ants. They camouflage themselves by attaching the sucked-out bodies of ants to their back by means of fine hairs and silk threads.
Length 1 inch (2.5 cm).

Assassin bug
(Acanthaspis sp.)

Common name
　Assassin
　bugs

Family Reduviidae

Suborder Heteroptera

Order Hemiptera

Class/Subphylum Insecta/Hexapoda

Number of species About 5,000 (106 U.S.)

Size From about 0.3 in (8 mm) to 1.6 in (4 cm)

Key features General shape oval to elongate, some actually resembling small stick insects; short, stout, curved, 3-segmented rostrum that fits in a groove beneath the thorax when not in use; noticeable groove across head behind the eyes; front legs adapted for clasping prey, so they usually walk on the hind 2 pairs; pronotum may have a crest or may bear spikes, which may also occur on top of the head

Habits Walk around on vegetation and on the ground in search of prey, often moving slowly and stealthily; blood-sucking species find their prey by flying in search of it; some species attract prey by using "tools" such as resin

Breeding Females of a number of species exhibit parental care, as do males in some species

Diet Other insects and their larvae; spiders; the blood of vertebrates; one species known to feed on liquid from fermenting dung

Habitat Many species live on vegetation, while others live on the ground or on tree bark; some species inhabit the nests of termites; found in all kinds of habitat—grassland, forests, marshes, and deserts

Distribution Worldwide, but with the greatest variety of species in the tropical regions

Stink Bugs

The bright colors of the shield bug *Catacanthus anchorago* from Asia give a clear indication to would-be predators that the bug contains foul-tasting defensive chemicals and gives off equally unpleasant smells. Length about 0.5 inches (13 mm).

Shield bug *(Catacanthus anchorago)*

Common name Stink bugs (shield bugs)

Family Pentatomidae

Suborder Heteroptera

Order Hemiptera

Class/Subphylum Insecta/Hexapoda

Number of species About 5,000 (222 U.S.)

Size From about 0.2 in (4 mm) to 1 in (2.5 cm)

Key features Broad-bodied, often oval-shaped bugs, nearly as wide as they are long; often rather flattened on top; scutellum is usually triangular, extending over as much as half the abdomen but not overlapping the membranous area of the forewings by much; front of the pronotum may have blunt or pointed projections on either side of the head; stink glands present

Habits Most often found on the plants on which they feed; predaceous species found on any suitable vegetation in search of prey

Breeding In a number of species the females care for their eggs and young; in many species males stridulate to attract females

Diet Many are sap feeders; others feed on insects, especially soft-bodied ones such as larvae

Habitat Meadows, grassland, forests, sand dunes, seashore, marshes, and deserts

Distribution Worldwide, but tropical zones are especially rich in species

Lanternflies

The lanternfly *Phenax variegata* from South America roosts on lichen-covered bark, which it resembles. It often has long filaments of wax protruding from the end of the abdomen. Length up to 1 inch (2.5 cm).

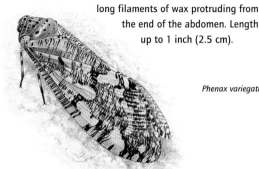

Phenax variegata

Common name Lanternflies (fulgorid bugs, fulgorid planthoppers)

Family Fulgoridae

Suborder Auchenorrhyncha

Order Hemiptera

Class/Subphylum Insecta/Hexapoda

Number of species About 700 (at least 1 U.S.)

Size From about 0.4 in (10 mm) to 4 in (10 cm)

Key features Both fore- and hind wings covered in a complicated network of veins and cross-veins; many (especially tropical) species have strange growths from the front of the head, sometimes knobbed or spiny; color may be plain browns or greens, or sometimes very colorful

Habits Like most plant feeders, they sit motionless on their host plant to escape detection by predators

Breeding Some species produce sounds during courtship; females of some species lay eggs into the ground

Diet Sap from their host plant species

Habitat Mainly forests

Distribution Usually found in the tropics; a few species in temperate zones

Spittlebugs

Cicadas

The meadow spittlebug, *Philaenus spumarius*, is found in North America and Europe. Shown here are two of the 11 color variations. Length about 0.2 inches (5–6 mm). *Cercopis vulnerata* is from Europe. Length 0.3–0.4 inches (9–11 mm).

Cicadas are sometimes kept in Asia for their song, as they were in ancient Greece. They are common around the Mediterranean region, where they favor pine trees. *Tibicen plebejus*, a European species, is around 1.2–1.5 inches (3–3.7 cm) in length.

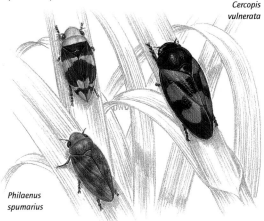

Cercopis vulnerata

Philaenus spumarius

Tibicen plebejus

Common name Spittlebugs (froghoppers, cuckoo-spit insects)

Family Cercopidae

Suborder Auchenorrhyncha

Order Hemiptera

Class/Subphylum Insecta/Hexapoda

Number of species About 2,400 (54 U.S.)

Size From about 0.12 in (3 mm) to 0.8 in (20 mm)

Key features Rather squat body shaped like a miniature frog, with powerful hind legs for jumping long distances in relation to body size; either brownish or with bright warning colors; forewings leathery and colored; tibiae cylindrical (unlike the similar-looking leafhoppers, which have tibiae with an angular cross section); nymphs easily recognizable, living in a mass of froth

Habits Normally found sitting on food plants; many adults not noticeable unless they jump

Breeding Females lay eggs in crevices on or near food plants, or directly into soil; some produce protective secretion around eggs

Diet Some adults feed from parts of plants growing above ground, as do many nymphs; others feed from plant roots

Habitat Meadows, gardens, grassland, moors, forests, mountains, and deserts

Distribution Worldwide, with many temperate species

Common name Cicadas

Family Cicadidae

Suborder Auchenorrhyncha

Order Hemiptera

Class/Subphylum Insecta/Hexapoda

Number of species About 1,500 (160 U.S.)

Size From about 0.4 in (10 mm) to 4 in (10 cm)

Key features Mainly large insects; both pairs of wings membranous and transparent, held over the body like a tent; males have sound-producing structures beneath the front end of the abdomen; body often green or brown and well camouflaged

Habits Most species live in trees or bushes from which males call to females; nymphs live beneath the ground and are not seen until they emerge to molt into adults; adults fly strongly

Breeding Male cicadas have a distinct "song" to attract females of their own species; females insert eggs into twigs

Diet Adults take sap from the trees on which they live; nymphs take sap from tree roots

Habitat Mainly forests and woodlands; also in deserts where suitable woody plants grow

Distribution Worldwide, but more common in tropical zones

Leafhoppers

The rhododendron leafhopper, *Graphocephala fennahi*, is found in the United States and Europe. Length 0.3-0.4 inches (8-10 mm). *Cicadella viridis* is from the Northern Hemisphere. Length 0.2-0.3 inches (6-8 mm). *Aphrodes bifasciatus* is the smallest of these three leafhoppers and lives in Europe. Length 0.1-0.15 inches (3-4 mm).

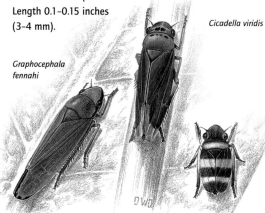

Cicadella viridis

Graphocephala fennahi

Aphrodes bifasciatus

Common name Leafhoppers

Family Cicadellidae

Suborder Auchenorrhyncha

Order Hempitera

Class/Subphylum Insecta/Hexapoda

Number of species About 20,000 (2,500 U.S.)

Size From about 0.08 in (2 mm) to 0.8 in (20 mm)

Key features Usually longer and slimmer than the spittlebugs they resemble, with an angular cross section to the tibiae; tibiae bear 1 or more rows of spines; forewings leathery, often brightly colored, distinguishing them from small cicadas

Habits Usually found on their food plants; winged species will readily fly to escape when disturbed

Breeding Many species stridulate to attract mates and during courtship, which may also involve "dance" routines; eggs laid in or on food plants

Diet All species suck sap from plants, often living on just 1 particular plant species; like aphids, they produce honeydew

Habitat Meadows, gardens, grassland, forests, marshes, mountains, and deserts

Distribution Worldwide, but more common in tropical zones

Whiteflies

The greenhouse whitefly, *Trialeurodes vaporariorum*, is a worldwide pest of tomatoes and houseplants. As well as sucking nutrients from the plants, the sugary honeydew excreted gets infested with fungi. Length 0.1 inches (2 mm).

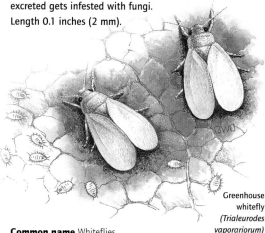

Greenhouse whitefly (*Trialeurodes vaporariorum*)

Common name Whiteflies

Family Aleyrodidae

Suborder Sternorrhyncha

Order Hemiptera

Class/Subphylum Insecta/Hexapoda

Number of species About 1,160 (100 U.S.)

Size Up to 0.1 in (2-2.5 mm)

Key features Tiny insects covered in a waxy powder that gives them a white appearance; membranous wings, which are white or mottled, held almost flat over the body, with slight overlap along the centerline; early nymphs have legs and can move around, later instars cannot use legs and remain in one place

Habits Often found in large numbers on food plants; nymphs cover the underside of leaves; adults fly readily with a weak flight when disturbed

Breeding Reproduction is sexual or by parthenogenesis; when courtship occurs, it can be complex; eggs laid singly or in batches; parental care has been recorded

Diet All species suck sap from host plants; a number are pests of cultivated plants

Habitat Forests, fields, plantations, and orchards

Distribution Worldwide, but more species in the warmer regions

Aphids

Found all over the world, the very common peach-potato aphid, *Myzus persicae*, feeds on more than 200 plants, including peaches and potatoes, on which it is a pest. As a carrier of the fungal disease potato blight, this species helped cause the Irish potato famine in the 1840s, which was responsible for the deaths of almost 1 million people. Length 0.07 inches (2 mm).

Peach-potato aphid
(*Myzus persicae*)

Common name Aphids

Family Aphididae

Suborder Sternorrhyncha

Order Hemiptera

Class/Subphylum Insecta/Hexapoda

Number of species About 3,800 (1,380 U.S.)

Size From about 0.04 in (1 mm) to 0.2 in (5 mm)

Key features Most commonly green or pink in color, but may be brown or black; females normally wingless; in males both pairs of wings transparent and folded tentlike over the body; body rather soft; abdomen with pair of cornicles on fifth or sixth abdominal segment

Habits Adults and nymphs usually found together in huge numbers on their host plants, on above-ground structures, or on plant roots

Breeding Life cycles can be very complex, including parthenogenesis and alternating of host plant species

Diet All suck the sap of plants, producing honeydew as a by-product; some species produce and live in galls

Habitat Forests, meadows, grassland, moorland, on waterside and floating plants, marshes, and seashore

Distribution Worldwide, but with the greater number of species in temperate regions

Scale Insects

The vine scale, *Parthenolecanium corni*, is a widespread plant pest. It damages the leaves and fruit of the plants it lives on due to the growth of a sooty mold on the honeydew produced by the bug. Length 0.2 inches (6 mm).

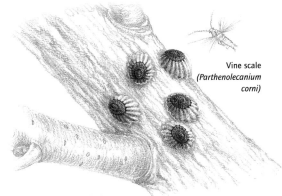

Vine scale
(*Parthenolecanium corni*)

Common name Scale insects
(soft, wax, and tortoise scales)

Family Coccidae

Suborder Sternorrhyncha

Order Hemiptera

Class/Subphylum Insecta/Hexapoda

Number of species About 1,000 (84 U.S.)

Size From about 0.04 in (1 mm) to 0.2 in (5 mm)

Key features Males and females look completely different; males lack mouthparts and have just 1 front pair of transparent, membranous wings, the 2nd pair resembling the halteres of the flies; alternatively, males may be wingless but still recognizable as insects; females may not resemble normal insects: the rostrum is present, but antennae are tiny or nonexistent; normal division of the body into segments not clear; top of the body is covered by a plate resembling a fish scale; wings absent; legs reduced and often nonworking; a powdery or waxy coating may also be present on the body

Habits Females most often found fixed in one place to any part of their host plant or plants, usually in quite large numbers

Breeding Females cannot fly and are sought out by the males; life cycles are quite complicated

Diet Females are sap feeders, often on a single plant species, and produce honeydew as a by-product

Habitat Grassland, forests, gardens, orchards, fields, and deserts

Distribution Worldwide, but more species are found in tropical regions

Ground Beetles

The European caterpillar hunter, *Calosoma sycophanta*, lives in gardens and woods. It has been introduced to parts of North America. Length up to 2 inches (5 cm).

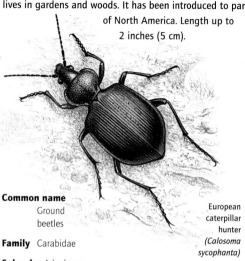

European caterpillar hunter (*Calosoma sycophanta*)

Common name Ground beetles

Family Carabidae

Suborder Adephaga

Order Coleoptera

Class/Subphylum Insecta/Hexapoda

Number of species About 25,000 (over 3,000 U.S.)

Size From about 0.1 in (3 mm) to 2.4 in (6 cm)

Key features Body mostly black, shiny, and metallic, often with a flush of purple or green iridescence over the ground color; so variable that no one characteristic is "typical"; a small number of brightly colored species; legs mostly long; jaws usually quite prominent; elytra usually with numerous furrows running lengthwise, often also pitted; antennae usually threadlike (sometimes beadlike); eyes usually large; often wingless

Habits Most are nocturnal; during the day usually found under stones, fallen logs, or among moss and fallen leaves, emerging at night to hunt for food

Breeding Mating not usually preceded by any kind of courtship; eggs mostly laid in the ground, sometimes in a special "nest"; adults often relatively long-lived, often 2–3 years, sometimes even 4 years

Diet Many species are predators of worms, snails, caterpillars, and other insects; a few species feed on seeds, fungi, pollen, and other vegetable matter; scavenging for dead insects probably common; larvae may be parasitic on other insect larvae

Habitat Common in gardens and woodlands, less so in more open habitats; many species on the seashore; several eyeless species in caves

Distribution Widespread around the world, except in the polar regions and the driest deserts

Diving Beetles

The great water beetle, *Dytiscus marginalis*, is found in European ponds and still water with plenty of vegetation. It is a voracious predator, including frogs, newts, and small fish in its diet. Length up to 1.4 inches (3.5 cm).

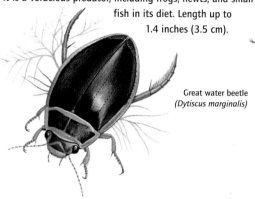

Great water beetle (*Dytiscus marginalis*)

Common name Diving beetles (water beetles)

Family Dytiscidae

Suborder Adephaga

Order Coleoptera

Class/Subphylum Insecta/Hexapoda

Number of species About 3,000 (about 475 U.S.)

Size Adults 0.06 in (1.5 mm) to 1.8 in (4.5 cm); larvae up to 2.7 in (7 cm)

Key features Adults mostly blackish or brownish with a streamlined elongate-oval shape, convex both at the top and on the underside; hind legs flattened as paddles and fringed with hairs; antennae quite long and threadlike; larvae long and narrow with conspicuous curved jaws

Habits Aquatic beetles that come to the surface to breathe air; both adults and larvae actively hunt prey in daytime; most adults can fly and will migrate in order to find new habitats

Breeding Mating takes place underwater; eggs are attached to underwater plants or laid inside them; larvae may pupate underwater or move to the shore to do so; in areas subject to drought both larvae and adults can survive dry periods by burrowing into mud

Diet Tadpoles, adult frogs, small fish, shrimp, worms, leeches, snails, and water mites; insects such as dragonfly and damselfly larvae; also cannibalistic

Habitat Streams, roadside ditches, ponds, lakes, and pools (including those that are stagnant or temporary); also in hot-water springs and salty pools on the coast

Distribution Worldwide except in the coldest or driest areas

Soldier Beetles

Cantharis rustica is a Northern Hemisphere soldier beetle. It is usually found on flowers, where it feeds on insects. The beetle is sometimes used by anglers as bait for trout. Body length up to 0.6 inches (15 mm).

Cantharis rustica

Common name Soldier beetles

Family Cantharidae

Suborder Polyphaga

Order Coleoptera

Class/Subphylum Insecta/Hexapoda

Number of species About 5,500 (about 460 U.S.)

Size Mainly in the range 0.4–0.6 in (10–15 mm)

Key features Body mainly black, brown, yellowish, or dull reddish color; often fairly narrow, almost parallel-sided, becoming slightly wider toward the rear end; elytra cover the abdomen only loosely; rather soft body compared with most beetles; antennae mostly long and threadlike, sometimes comblike or sawtoothed; head plainly visible from above; larvae often densely bristly

Habits Adults often conspicuous, feeding in large numbers on flowers or perched on foliage, seldom moving far or fast; larvae mainly carnivorous, rarely seen, living beneath loose bark, under fallen logs, or in damp ground

Breeding Mating takes place in daytime, often on flowers or leaves and may last many hours or even days; males often fight for possession of females, who will sometimes cannibalize their mates during copulation

Diet Adults feed on nectar, pollen, or soft-bodied insects; larvae mainly carnivorous, feeding primarily on soft-bodied helpless prey such as insect eggs, fly maggots, and small caterpillars

Habitat Grasslands, hedgerows, gardens, forests, and mountainsides; rarely in deserts

Distribution Worldwide, but commonest in temperate areas

Fireflies

The wingless, larvalike female of the firefly *Lampyris noctiluca* has light-producing organs that are carried in her last three abdominal segments. This European species of grassland firefly reaches 0.6 inches (15 mm) in length.

♀ *Lampyris noctiluca*

Common name Fireflies (lightning bugs)

Family Lampyridae

Suborder Polyphaga

Order Coleoptera

Class/Subphylum Insecta/Hexapoda

Number of species About 2,000 (about 136 U.S.)

Size From about 0.2 in (5 mm) to about 0.8 in (20 mm)

Key features Body drab brown or blackish; when viewed from above, head is more or less concealed beneath the pronotum, which is also very broad (almost as broad as the elytra); body soft and flattened with sides generally parallel; females often with short wings or wingless and larvalike (larviform); antennae threadlike or often sawtoothed; luminous organ usually present on tip of abdomen

Habits All larvae and most adults are luminescent; light production takes place only during the night; by day the adults rest on foliage and are inconspicuous

Breeding Males fly around flashing their lights at night; the perched females reply with their own lights, acting as a beacon to which the males can easily fly for mating; some species are not luminescent or only weakly so and are active in daytime

Diet The adults of most species apparently do not feed; females of some species attract and feed on males of unrelated species; the larvae are carnivorous, feeding on insect larvae, mites, snails, and slugs

Habitat Mainly in forests; also in grasslands, gardens, riversides, and swamps

Distribution Worldwide, avoiding very cold or dry areas; most abundant in the tropics

Jewel Beetles

Ladybugs

Females of the jewel beetle *Anthaxia nitidula* are mainly found on flowers, especially yellow ones. The larvae develop under trees and shrubs such as almond and rose. Length up to 0.3 inches (8 mm).

♀ *Anthaxia nitidula*

A seven-spot ladybug, *Coccinella 7-punctata*, in flight revealing its true wings under its hardened and colorful elytra. Length up to 0.3 inches (8 mm).

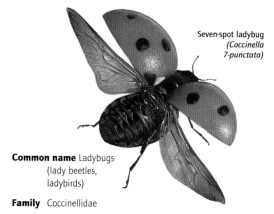

Seven-spot ladybug
(*Coccinella 7-punctata*)

Common name Jewel beetles (metallic wood-boring beetles, splendor beetles)

Family Buprestidae

Suborder Polyphaga

Order Coleoptera

Class/Subphylum Insecta/Hexapoda

Number of species About 13,000 (about 720 U.S.)

Size From about 0.1 in (3 mm) to about 3 in (8 cm)

Key features Mainly brightly colored, often metallic, sometimes densely hairy; body hard, usually deep and bullet shaped, with a broad head and thorax, tapering off rapidly toward the rear; antennae short, often inconspicuous, usually sawtoothed, also comblike or threadlike

Habits Adults fly rapidly in bright sunshine, bask on leaves or tree trunks, or feed on flowers; females often found on dead and dying trees

Breeding Mating mainly takes place on the dead and dying trees inhabited by the larvae, and in which eggs are generally laid; males may be attracted to females visually or through the release of pheromones

Diet Some adults seldom, if ever, feed; others feed on pollen, nectar, or plant material; larvae mainly feed inside the stems of plants, especially the trunks and branches of trees; some form galls or leaf mines on plants

Habitat Mainly forests, although many spectacular kinds are restricted to deserts and mountains

Distribution Commonest in the tropics, but also found far to the north and south; *Agrilus* is found worldwide and is probably the largest genus of living organisms, with several thousand species

Common name Ladybugs (lady beetles, ladybirds)

Family Coccinellidae

Suborder Polyphaga

Order Coleoptera

Class/Subphylum Insecta/Hexapoda

Number of species About 4,500 (about 400 U.S.)

Size From about 0.04 in (1 mm) to about 0.4 in (10 mm)

Key features Mainly brightly colored red or yellow, usually spotted or blotched with black; distinctive oval or almost round body, noticeably dome shaped on top and flattened beneath; antennae short and weakly clubbed; head hardly visible from above

Habits Mainly active during the day on plants, where adults and larvae of many species are beneficial in eating pests; some species hibernate in huge swarms

Breeding Males usually mate without any courtship; males guard females in some species; females of predatory species lay batches of eggs near aphids; larvae highly mobile and actively move around in quest for prey; pupa (with no appendages visible) attached by rear end to some form of support

Diet Many species feed on aphids; others prefer scale insects, mealybugs, mites, and other soft-bodied invertebrates and their eggs; some species are vegetarian and may damage crops; others graze on molds growing on leaves

Habitat Gardens, fields, orchards, hedgerows, forests, and mountainsides; rarely in deserts

Distribution Worldwide except in the driest and coldest regions; commonest in temperate countries

Stag Beetles

A pair of male European stag beetles, *Lucanus cervus*, spar for the attention of a female; the stronger one usually wins this pushing and shoving match. Length up to 3 inches (7.5 cm).

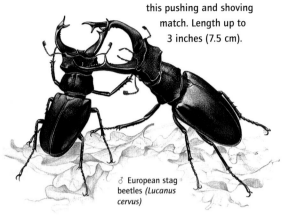

♂ European stag beetles *(Lucanus cervus)*

Common name Stag beetles (pinching bugs)

Family Lucanidae

Suborder Polyphaga

Order Coleoptera

Class/Subphylum Insecta/Hexapoda

Number of species About 1,250 (about 30 U.S.)

Size From about 0.3 in (8 mm) to about 3.5 in (9 cm)

Key features Body mainly large and black, brown, or reddish-brown; sometimes yellow or green, usually shiny; antennae distinctive, elbowed, with a comblike terminal club whose plates cannot be held together (unlike in scarabs); male jaws often large and antlerlike; many species flightless

Habits Adults mainly nocturnal, often flying to lights, sometimes in large numbers

Breeding Males use antlerlike jaws in fights to gain access to females; eggs are laid in cracks in the bark of dead trees or stumps; larvae of larger species take at least 5 years to pupate; it is then a further year before the adults emerge

Diet Adults feed on aphid honeydew and sap leaking from trees; a few feed on flowers; some species probably do not feed as adults; larvae eat wood inside trees

Habitat Mainly woodland; also in gardens, city lots, and city streets that are lined with old trees; absent from areas with no sizable trees

Distribution Worldwide, except in very dry or cold areas

Long-Horned Beetles

A male harlequin beetle, *Acrocinus longimanus*, guards an egg-laying female. This giant species can be found from Mexico to Argentina. Its large body can measure up to 7 inches (18 cm) long.

♀

♂

Harlequin beetle *(Acrocinus longimanus)*

Common name Long-horned beetles

Family Cerambycidae

Suborder Polyphaga

Order Coleoptera

Class/Subphylum Insecta/Hexapoda

Number of species About 35,000 (about 1,250 U.S.)

Size From about 0.2 in (5 mm) to about 8 in (20 cm)

Key features Variously colored, often brown or black; many black with yellow bands or stripes, some brightly colored, sometimes metallic; antennae normally at least half the length of the body, frequently at least as long as the body and sometimes much longer; antennae generally threadlike, sometimes feathery; eyes usually with a distinct notch; body long and fairly narrow

Habits Many adults active in daytime and found on flowers in bright sunshine; others nocturnal; many nocturnal species are well camouflaged while resting on tree trunks during the day; larvae mostly bore in wood

Breeding Mating often takes place on flowers or diseased trees; courtship usually absent; females may treat males roughly, biting off antennae; males spend long periods "riding" on females until they lay their eggs; eggs usually laid in dead or living trees, sometimes with elaborate preparations by female, such as the "girdling" of living twigs

Diet Adults feed mainly on pollen; some prefer sap or feed on fruit, fungi, or leaves, while others do not feed at all; larvae eat wood or roots

Habitat Mainly forests; also in grasslands, swamps, deserts, and gardens

Distribution Worldwide, but commonest in the tropics

Scarab Beetles

Weevils

Giant among beetles, male Hercules beetles, *Dynastes hercules*, from Central and South America fight using their horns as pry bars to topple each other over and off tree trunks. Length up to
7 inches (18 cm).

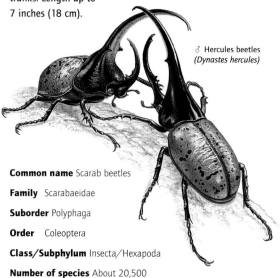

♂ Hercules beetles
(*Dynastes hercules*)

Common name Scarab beetles

Family Scarabaeidae

Suborder Polyphaga

Order Coleoptera

Class/Subphylum Insecta/Hexapoda

Number of species About 20,500
(about 1,380 U.S.)

Size From about 0.2 in (4 mm) to about 7 in (18 cm)

Key features Body usually stout and heavy, oval or oval-elongate, often brightly colored, especially in the tropics; antennae unique, elbowed, and tipped with a series of flat, elongated leaflike plates (lamellae) that can be separated by opening them up like a fan or closed to form a club; a few species have divided eyes

Habits Enormously varied; some are associated with dung, some with flowers, and others with roots or leaves; many species only active at dusk or after dark, others only in warm sunshine

Breeding Many species have horned males that fight over access to females; some species form "balls" of males scuffling over a single female; male chafers tend to form aerial swarms to attract females; dung-rolling beetles collect dung, others make a "compost" from plant material; many species lay eggs in trees or roots

Diet Larvae feed on dung, leaves, fruit, roots, wood, fungi, carrion, fur, and bones; many adults only eat pollen and nectar

Habitat Almost anywhere; as common in deserts and pastures as in forests or gardens; some species inhabit the nests of mammals, birds, or termites

Distribution More or less throughout the world wherever insect life is possible on dry land

The acorn weevil, *Curculio venosus*, is found in southern England and Europe. Length 0.2–0.4 inches (5–9 mm). *Phytonomus nigrirostris* is from Europe and the U.S., where it is known as the cloverleaf weevil. Length 0.1–0.2 inches (3–4 mm).

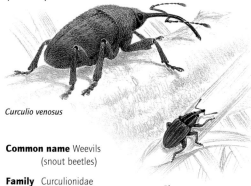

Curculio venosus

Common name Weevils
(snout beetles)

Family Curculionidae

Suborder Polyphaga

Order Coleoptera

Phytonomus nigrirostris

Class/Subphylum Insecta/Hexapoda

Number of species About 50,000 (about 2,500 U.S.)

Size From about 0.04 in (1 mm) to about 3 in (7.5 cm)

Key features Color very variable: brown, black, yellow, orange, red, blue, purple, green, gold, or silver; body often covered with iridescent scales; some species very hairy; downcurved snout usually well developed, sometimes broad and flat, more often longer (sometimes very long) and slimmer; antennae usually elbowed, tipped by a 3-segmented club; elytra often fused

Habits Adults are usually seen on vegetation; mostly active in daytime; larvae usually live concealed inside roots, stems, or galls

Breeding Male simply mounts female; in some species males conduct ritualistic "fights"; mating is often lengthy, and males often remain with females as "escorts" until egg laying starts; females drill hole in plant with rostrum before laying an egg in the hole; many species restricted to a single host plant; leaf-rolling weevils construct living "leaf cradles"

Diet Adults mainly eat pollen or leaves; larvae usually eat plant tissues within stems, roots, galls, fruits, or seeds; some feed externally on leaves, often in groups; 1 species eats dung, at least 1 other feeds on insect eggs

Habitat Most common in forests, but some prefer open habitats such as grasslands or deserts; larvae of some species live in aquatic plants, others inhabit rodent burrows or ants' nests

Distribution Worldwide except in the coldest and driest areas

Swallowtail Butterflies

Queen Alexandra's birdwing, *Ornithoptera alexandrae*, is found to the east of the Owen Stanley Ranges in southeast New Guinea. It is one of seven protected butterfly species on the island. Wingspan 6.6–11 inches (17–28 cm).

Queen Alexandra's birdwing *(Ornithoptera alexandrae)*

Common name Swallowtail butterflies (apollos, swordtails, birdwings)

Family Papilionidae

Order Lepidoptera

Class/Subphylum Insecta/Hexapoda

Number of species About 550 (27 U.S.)

Wingspan From about 1.2 in (3 cm) to about 11 in (28 cm)

Key features Mainly large butterflies (including the world's largest), often with hind-wing tails; colors varied, often consisting of just 2 colors, such as black and yellow or black and green, sometimes with red or blue spots; some species (apollos) have semitransparent wings; antennae knobbed but never with hooked tips; all 6 adult legs of equal size; caterpillars often with "Y"-shaped defensive osmeterium

Habits Adults feed on flowers or on salty ground, where they form large aggregations; caterpillars mainly feed singly

Breeding Male and female of most species look very similar; many males use pheromones from androconial scales during courtship; eggs spherical, usually laid singly; caterpillars with smooth skins, often with knobby projections; pupa suspended upright from silken girdle

Diet Adults feed on flowers, damp ground, or dung; caterpillars eat leaves belonging to plants of many families, including poisonous *Aristolochia* vines

Habitat Commonest in tropical rain forest, but found in many temperate habitats such as swamps, parks, and gardens; some species found only on high mountains or open tundra in the far north

Distribution Worldwide, occurring as far north as Alaska

Whites

The orange sulfur, *Colias eurytheme*, is a common North American species. Its favored host plant of alfalfa gives it the alternative common name of the alfalfa butterfly. Wingspan 1.5–2.4 inches (4–6 cm).

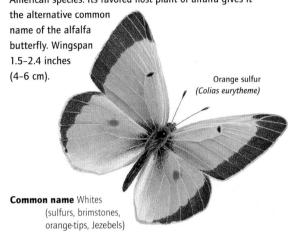

Orange sulfur *(Colias eurytheme)*

Common name Whites (sulfurs, brimstones, orange-tips, Jezebels)

Family Pieridae

Order Lepidoptera

Class/Subphylum Insecta/Hexapoda

Number of species About 1,500 (58 U.S.)

Wingspan From about 0.9 in (23 mm) to about 4 in (10 cm)

Key features Wings mainly with broadly rounded tips; wing color often white or yellow, sometimes with orange or red tips or even (in tropical species) with a brilliant colorful pattern; all 6 legs functional; caterpillar cylindrical, usually smooth and slender, often green; chrysalis supported by both cremaster and silken girdle

Habits Adults spend much time in flight, usually in open, sunny places; males of certain species congregate in large numbers to drink on riverside sand; a few species migratory

Breeding Sexes often look different—males normally brighter; some species with quite complex courtship involving both scent and sight; in most species males patrol in search of females, which often adopt specialized deterring posture

Diet Adults feed on nectar or on urine-soaked ground; caterpillars eat plants of a wide variety of families; some species are widespread pests of cultivated plants

Habitat Mainly open places such as grasslands, deserts, roadsides, gardens, and woodland clearings; many species are specialists on high mountains; numerous brightly colored species in tropical rain forests

Distribution Worldwide except Antarctica

Brush-Footed Butterflies

The red admiral, *Vanessa atalanta*, is a wide-ranging migratory butterfly that can be found almost anywhere there are flowers and ripe fruit. Adults are particularly fond of overripe and fermenting fruit.

Wingspan 1.2 inches (3 cm).

Red Admiral
(Vanessa atalanta)

Common name Brush-footed butterflies

Family Nymphalidae

Order Lepidoptera

Class/Subphylum Insecta/Hexapoda

Number of species About 3,000 (125 U.S.)

Wingspan From about 1 in (2.5 cm) to about 3.5 in (9 cm)

Key features Colors bright and varied, often very flamboyant and beautiful; wing shape diverse, sometimes with frilly edges; some species with tailed hind wings; front legs in both sexes reduced to form tiny brushlike appendages, leaving only 4 walking legs; none of the veins at base of wings greatly swollen; caterpillars smooth, hairy, or spiky

Habits Adults usually found on flowers or feeding on damp ground; most species are fast fliers; some species strongly migratory; in temperate regions overwintering may occur in adult stage; caterpillars solitary or gregarious

Diet Adults feed on flower nectar, fruit, fermenting tree sap, animal dung, urine-soaked ground, putrid animal corpses, and human sweat; caterpillars eat green leaves

Breeding Male and female usually look alike, but sometimes look very different; adults often engage in "spiraling" courtship; females may release pheromones to attract males; eggs laid singly or in masses; caterpillars often very spiny, but smooth and green in many tropical species; pupa suspended upside down from its tail, often with silver or gold spots

Habitat In all habitats, but most common in tropical rain forest; many species among the commonest butterflies in gardens, others restricted to high mountain slopes

Distribution Worldwide, occurring north as far as Greenland

Morphos

The blue morpho butterfly, *Morpho menelaus*, is found in the rain forests of South and Central America. When the male folds its blue wings, predators are fooled by the bark-colored underside.
Wingspan about 6 inches (15 cm).

♂ *Morpho menelaus*

Common name Morphos

Family Morphidae

Order Lepidoptera

Class/Subphylum Insecta/Hexapoda

Number of species About 50 (none U.S.)

Wingspan From about 3 in (7.5 cm) to about 6 in (15 cm)

Key features Adults very large; underside usually brown with rows of eyespots, upper side often brilliant shining metallic blue; some species shining pearly white, a few brown or blackish; 4 walking legs; caterpillars with conspicuous hair tufts and forked tail

Habits Adult males generally fly actively around in forest, often following rivers; normally perch with wings closed to reveal underside with eyespots

Breeding Males and females often different colors; males patrol along a beat looking for females; mating seldom seen; dome-shaped eggs are laid singly or in large batches; caterpillars feed singly or in groups

Diet Adults feed mostly on rotting fruit on the forest floor, but also on leaking tree sap, decaying fungi, carrion, and mud; larvae eat leaves of plants belonging to 6 different families

Habitat Mostly in lowland tropical rain forest, occasionally in drier forest and open, quite dry lower slopes of mountains

Distribution Tropical regions of Central and South America, from Mexico to northern Argentina

Milkweed Butterflies

Skippers

Danaus plexippus, the American monarch, is the only butterfly that migrates annually both northward and southward. It forms spectacular overwintering roosts, the largest being in the mountain forests in the state of Michoacán in Central Mexico. Wingspan 3.5–4 inches (9–10 cm).

American monarch
(Danaus plexippus)

Common name
Milkweed butterflies

Family Danaidae

Order Lepidoptera

Class/Subphylum Insecta/Hexapoda

Number of species About 250 (5 U.S.)

Wingspan From about 2 in (5 cm) to about 6 in (15 cm)

Key features Color range restricted, often brownish-orange spotted with black and white; some pale blue or lemon marked with black; a few lacelike, black and white, others very dark brown, sometimes with blue patches; wings generally broad; antennae without scales; 4 walking legs; larvae have fleshy outgrowths

Habits Adults are powerful fliers and include the most migratory of butterflies; 1 species (the monarch) overwinters in huge aggregations; all species often seen on flowers

Breeding Males generally have large hair pencils that release pheromones during courtship; males procure sexual pheromones by feeding on certain withered plants; eggs are flattened domes with prominent ribs; pupae sometimes covered with gold or silver spots, or may even be mirrorlike

Diet Adults feed on nectar from flowers; caterpillars eat toxic plants, mainly milkweeds and frangipani plants

Habitat In all habitats from deserts to mountains and from gardens to city lots

Distribution Mainly tropical, only reaching northern temperate areas by migrating northward in summer

The large skipper, *Ochlodes venata*, is found in Europe and Japan. Wingspan 1.4 inches (3.5 cm). The beautiful long-tailed skipper, *Urbanus proteus* from the southern United States and South America, is considered a pest by farmers and gardeners, who call it the "bean-leaf roller." Wingspan 1.5–2 inches (4–5 cm).

Ochlodes venata

Common name
Skippers

Family Hesperiidae

Order Lepidoptera

Class/Subphylum Insecta/Hexapoda

Number of species About 3,500 (263 U.S.)

Wingspan From 0.8 in (19 mm) to 3.5 in (9 cm)

Key features Body usually plump, hairy, and mothlike; head broad; antennae and eyes set far apart on head; antennae ending in short hook; wings short; color varied—in temperate areas mainly brownish or yellowish, in tropics often beautifully marked with green, scarlet, or blue; some species whitish; hind wings sometimes tailed

Habits Flight rapid and darting, quite unlike any other butterflies; adults often perch with forewings folded flat on each side of the body and hind wings horizontal—a unique habit; a few species active at dusk; at least 1 species nocturnal, all others day-active

Breeding Both sexes may have scent patches on wings, some males have hair pencils on legs; males mainly perch to await females, but some patrol; caterpillar usually smooth, normally with constriction behind neck, often living in rolled-up tube of host plant; pupa smooth, often formed inside a partial silk cocoon within the larval nest

Diet Adults feed on flowers, dung, sap, or muddy ground; caterpillars feed on a wide range of plants, often grasses in temperate species

Habitat In all habitats from deserts and grasslands to mountainsides and rain forests

Distribution Worldwide except in very cold or dry areas, occurring far north into Alaska

Sphinx Moths

Charles Darwin predicted the existence of the Madagascan hawk moth, *Xanthopan morgani praedicta*, before any specimens were ever found. That was because the orchid *Angraecum sesquipedale*, with its long floral spur, had to have a pollinator with an equally long tongue. Wingspan 5.1–5.9 inches (13–15 cm); proboscis 10 inches (25 cm).

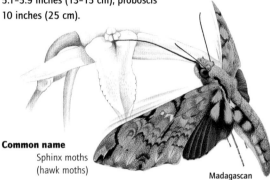

Madagascan hawk moth
(*Xanthopan morgani praedicta*)

Common name
Sphinx moths (hawk moths)

Family Sphingidae

Order Lepidoptera

Class/Subphylum Insecta/Hexapoda

Number of species About 1,000 (about 124 U.S.)

Wingspan From 0.4 in (10 mm) to about 8 in (20 cm)

Key features Body large, heavy, and tapering almost to a point at the rear; forewings long and narrow, much larger than hind wings; forewings and hind wings often different colors (forewings brown, grayish, pinkish, or green; hindwings pink, yellow, black and white, or other bright patterns); antennae thickened; proboscis generally long, sometimes very long; hearing organs absent; caterpillar with hornlike "tail"

Habits Adults fastest fliers of all moths, with very rapid wing beat; most species active at night, adults mostly seen when visiting flowers, with rapid "zoom-hover" style of flight

Breeding Males and females generally look similar, but males are smaller and have a pair of scent brushes on the abdomen; females lay eggs singly while hovering over food plant; caterpillars shiny, wrinkled, and often with stripes or eyespots; pupa often with conspicuous proboscis, normally naked, without cocoon; pupa usually placed in soil

Diet Adults feed on flowers, rotting fruit, fermenting tree sap, or honey; caterpillars eat leaves of living plants; some are pests of crops and cultivated plants

Habitat In all habitats, but most common in tropical rain forests; some species breed in gardens or even on roadside trees in city centers

Distribution Worldwide, but mostly tropical

Giant Silkworm Moths

Attacus edwardsi is one of a small number of atlas moths—the giants of the moth world. Atlas moths come from Asia; however, the population may be under threat because of the interest of collectors. Wingspan up to 12 inches (30 cm).

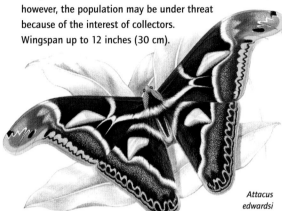

Attacus edwardsi

Common name Giant silkworm moths (royal moths, emperor moths)

Family Saturniidae

Order Lepidoptera

Class/Subphylum Insecta/Hexapoda

Number of species About 1,100 (69 U.S.)

Wingspan From about 1.2 in (3 cm) to about 14 in (36 cm)

Key features Colors varied, often bright and attractive; forewings usually relatively long and narrow, tapering toward tip; hind wings often with spots or tails; wings held out to sides of body when at rest; frenulum absent; head small; body densely hairy; proboscis reduced in size or absent; antennae simple to pectinate in females, usually larger and strongly pectinate in males; hearing organs absent; caterpillar fleshy, usually with bristles or stinging spines

Habits Adults mostly nocturnal; a few species active by day or at dusk; nocturnal species easily attracted to lights; caterpillars may sit in conspicuous groups

Breeding Females release pheromones that can be detected by large feathery antennae of males over great distances; some species conduct visual courtship by day; eggs laid either singly, in small groups, or large masses depending on species

Diet Adults do not feed; caterpillars feed on wide variety of leaves, mainly from trees

Habitat Most common in forests, but also in gardens, city lots, on mountainsides, and open places in general

Distribution Worldwide, but most common in the tropics

Tiger Moths

The great tiger moth (also known as the garden tiger moth), *Arctia caja*, is found throughout the Northern Hemisphere. Its appearance is so variable that it is rare to find two individuals with the same markings. Wingspan 1.8–2.6 inches (4.5–6.5 cm).

Great tiger moth
(*Arctia caja*)

Common name Tiger moths

Family Arctiidae

Order Lepidoptera

Class/Subphylum Insecta/Hexapoda

Number of species About 10,000 (264 U.S.)

Wingspan From 0.5 in (13 mm) to about 3.2 in (8 cm)

Key features Adults often among the most brightly colored of all moths; may also be white, or drab brown or gray; wing shape very varied, sometimes long and narrow, otherwise relatively broad; proboscis often reduced in size; antennae in male pectinate or simple, always simple in female; hearing organs present on thorax; some species mimic other insects; caterpillars generally very hairy, some known as woolly bears

Habits Adults either nocturnal or day-active (diurnal); diurnal species often very active, feeding and mating by day; may be very prominent in localized colonies

Breeding Courtship very complex; several species form large groups (leks) for mating by day or night; males may inflate large sacs called coremata; some derive pheromones by feeding on certain plants; eggs laid in masses or scattered randomly over vegetation; caterpillars pupate in loose cocoon formed from silk mixed with their own hairs

Diet Adults of many species do not feed; others feed by day or night on flowers; caterpillars feed on lichens or a wide variety of plants

Habitat Found in all habitats from coastal sandhills and saltmarshes to deserts, grasslands, forests, and mountainsides; some species most common in gardens

Distribution Worldwide, but most abundant in the tropics

Tussock Moths

Lymantria monacha, the black arches, is common across most of northern and central Europe and is found in parts of Asia and Japan. Wingspan 1.4–2.2 inches (3.5–5.5 cm).

Black arches
(*Lymantria monacha*)

Common name Tussock moths

Family Lymantriidae

Order Lepidoptera

Class/Subphylum Insecta/Hexapoda

Number of species About 2,500 (32 U.S.)

Wingspan From about 0.8 in (20 mm) to about 2.8 in (7 cm)

Key features Adults stout and hairy; wings mostly brownish or grayish; usually drab, but some tropical species brightly colored; some females have only stublike wings; wings generally held tentlike over the back; proboscis reduced in size or absent; antennae conspicuous and doubly pectinate in both male and female, but more so in male; females larger than males; females of some species wingless (sometimes without legs as well) or with poorly developed wings and unable to fly; caterpillars often brightly colored and generally hairy, causing a severe itching rash in humans

Habits Adults short-lived; nocturnal, hiding away during the day and seldom seen; caterpillars mostly found singly on leaves of food plant

Breeding Eggs usually deposited in dense masses, often covered with tufts of hair from the female's abdomen; pupa formed within loose cocoon of silk, often incorporating larval hairs

Diet Adults nonfeeding; caterpillars mostly eat foliage of trees and can be major pests

Habitat Mainly in woodland and forest; some species common in gardens

Distribution Worldwide; commonest in tropical regions of the Old World

Ichneumon Wasps

Gasteruption jaculator (family Gasteruptiidae) has the common name of banner wasp and is found in northern and central Europe. Like many species of parasitic wasps, its larvae feed on the larvae of solitary bees. Body length 0.6 inches (15 mm).

Banner wasp
(Gasteruption jaculator)

Common name Ichneumon wasps

Family Ichneumonidae

Division Parasitica

Suborder Apocrita

Order Hymenoptera

Class/Subphylum Insecta/Hexapoda

Number of species About 60,000 (about 12,000 U.S.)

Size From about 0.1 in (3 mm) to about 3 in (7.5 cm)

Key features Body often long and slender, usually black, often with red, white, or yellow markings; female may have long needlelike ovipositor; long, constantly moving antennae with 13 or more segments, often tipped white; adults usually fully winged, but occasionally with shortened wings or none at all

Habits Adults often found on flowers or walking across foliage searching for hosts; larvae are parasites on other invertebrates, mainly insects

Breeding Little is known about mating habits in most species; in some species mating occurs on the tree trunks from which the adults emerged; females seek out hosts such as caterpillars in which to lay eggs; certain species can penetrate solid bark to lay eggs in larvae burrowing within; ichneumon larvae consume their living host, eventually killing it

Diet Adults feed on nectar, aphid honeydew, or liquids leaking from host, often from punctures made by the ovipositor; larvae feed parasitically on living invertebrates, especially caterpillars of Lepidoptera; a few feed on plant products stored by host

Habitat In all terrestrial habitats; most common in temperate forests and grassland, rare in arid zones

Distribution Worldwide except in very dry or cold areas

Gall Wasps

Diplolepis rosae, the European gall wasp, makes a "robin pincushion" gall on the wild rose.
Body length 0.2 inches (5 mm).

Diplolepis rosae

Common name Gall wasps

Family Cynipidae

Division Parasitica

Suborder Apocrita

Order Hymenoptera

Class/Subphylum Insecta/Hexapoda

Number of species Over 2,000 (over 200 U.S.)

Size From about 0.08 in (2 mm) to about 0.3 in (8 mm)

Key features Body black or dark brown, glossy, with humpbacked profile; abdomen of female flattened from side to side; wings with only a small number of veins; some species wingless; antennae long with 13 or 14 segments in females, 14 or 15 in males

Habits Adults small, secretive, and seldom seen; larvae form galls, which can be highly conspicuous on plants

Breeding Females lay eggs in plant tissues, usually restricting their attacks to just a single species of host plant; the plant responds by forming a gall in which the larvae feed

Diet Adults feed on nectar or honeydew or not at all; larvae mostly feed on plants, a few on other insects

Habitat Common in all terrestrial habitats, including deserts, from ground level to the tops of trees

Distribution Worldwide, but they avoid the driest and coldest zones

Digger Wasps

The largest of the European hymenopterans, the yellow-faced digger wasp, *Scolia flavifrons* from southern Europe, is harmless to humans. However, it is a parasite on the beetle *Oryctes nasicornis*. Body length 1.6 inches (4 cm).

Yellow-faced digger wasp *(Scolia flavifrons)*

Common name
Digger wasps

Family Scoliidae

Suborder Apocrita

Order Hymenoptera

Class/Subphylum Insecta/Hexapoda

Number of species About 300 (about 20 U.S.)

Size From about 0.5 in (13 mm) to about 2.4 in (6 cm)

Key features Mostly large, robustly built, hairy wasps; color usually black marked with brown, orange, or yellow; both sexes fully winged; female antennae 12-segmented, male antennae 13-segmented; outer sections of forewings have a corrugated appearance

Habits Adults mainly found on flowers in bright sunshine; larvae live underground on beetle larvae

Breeding Males considerably smaller and slimmer than females; males and females perform a "mating dance"; female digs into ground and lays egg on large beetle larvae

Diet Adults feed on flower nectar; larvae feed on living beetle larvae

Habitat Open countryside, meadows, mountainsides, coastal sand dunes, gardens, and woodland edges

Distribution Mainly in warmer parts of world; in North America as far north as southern Canada

Ants

Solenopsis geminata, the North American fire ant, is a serious crop pest. The common name derives from the burning sensation caused by the ants' venomous bites. Body length 0.03–0.2 inches (1–6 mm).

Fire ant *(Solenopsis geminata)*

Common name Ants

Family Formicidae

Suborder Apocrita

Order Hymenoptera

Class/Subphylum Insecta/Hexapoda

Number of species About 15,000 (about 600 U.S.)

Size From about 0.04 in (1 mm) to about 1.4 in (3.5 cm)

Key features Body usually black, brown, reddish, or yellowish; eyes small; antennae elbowed; waist (known as a pedicel) with one or two beadlike or scalelike segments; stinger may be present; wings absent in workers—usually present in sexual forms, but discarded later

Habits All ants are fully social, often constructing very large nests containing thousands of individuals; some species live in the nests of others or take other species as slaves

Breeding Most species release large numbers of winged males and females, which form nuptial swarms; after mating, queens break off their wings and establish new nest, usually without help of male, who normally dies (unlike in termites, where male becomes "king" alongside his "queen"); queen ant stores all sperm needed for fertilizing many eggs over a long period

Diet Adults feed mainly on nectar and honeydew or on fungus; larvae eat food of animal (mainly insect) or plant (mainly seed) origin; sole diet for some species is a fungus that they cultivate in special "gardens"

Habitat Found in all terrestrial habitats, where they are often dominant; no aquatic species

Distribution Worldwide; commonest in the tropics, absent from very dry or cold areas.

Social Wasps

The yellow jacket, *Vespula germanica* (also known as the German wasp), builds its nest in suitable buildings or underground and is common in Europe. Body length (of worker) 0.9 inches (22 mm).

Yellow jacket
(Vespula germanica)

Common name
    Social wasps
    (paper wasps, potter wasps)

Family Vespidae

Suborder Apocrita

Order Hymenoptera

Class/Subphylum Insecta/Hexapoda

Number of species About 4,000 (about 415 U.S.)

Size From about 0.2 in (5 mm) to about 1.4 in (3.5 cm)

Key features Body usually banded, often black and yellow or black and white; sometimes all black or brown, occasionally green; eyes with a distinct notch at the front; both sexes fully winged; pronotum reaches back to the wing bases; wings pleated when held at rest over back; females armed with stinger

Habits Mostly active during the day, a few species nocturnal; adults hunt for larval food on leaves or flowers; paper wasp nests often conspicuous on buildings; potter wasps may be conspicuous collecting mud around puddles

Breeding Potter wasps are solitary and build mud nests, which they fill with spiders; paper wasps are highly social; nests often large, usually made of "paper," in which overlapping generations of workers care for the young and eventually rear males and future queens; nests may be founded and dominated by one or more queens

Diet Adults mainly eat nectar from flowers, honeydew, juices oozing from ripe fruits, and leaking sap on tree trunks; larvae are mainly carnivorous

Habitat Common in all kinds of terrestrial habitats that are not too dry or cold

Distribution Worldwide, commonest in the tropics

Leaf-Cutter Bees and Relatives

The European wool-carder bee, *Anthidium manicatum*, builds its nest in cavities in wood or masonry, lining it with a cottonlike fluff "carded" from the leaves and stems of hairy plants. Body length of female 0.4 inches (10 mm); male 0.6 inches (15 mm).

♂ Wool-carder bee
(Anthidium manicatum)

Common name
    Leaf-cutter bees
    (leaf-cutting bees),
    mason bees, wool-carder bees

Family Megachilidae

Suborder Apocrita

Order Hymenoptera

Class/Subphylum Insecta/Hexapoda

Number of species Over 3,500 (about 600 U.S.)

Size From 0.4 in (10 mm) to 1.6 in (4 cm)

Key features Body stoutly built, usually hairy; gray or brown, sometimes boldly marked in black and yellow or black and orange; pollen carried on brush of hairs (scopa) on the underside of the abdomen, rather than on the hind legs as in most other bees; tongue long and slender

Habits Usually seen collecting pollen from flowers, cutting leaves or gathering other materials to line nests, or digging nests in ground; some species are cuckoos in nests of others

Breeding Males of some species are territorial around flowers or nests; females build nests in tunnels in the ground or in natural cavities in wood or stone; leaf-cutter females cut sections of leaf with which to build cells; mason bees build cells with mud; wool-carder bees collect fluffy plant material or animal hairs as nest-lining materials

Diet Adults feed on nectar from a variety of flowers; larvae feed on pollen and nectar collected by adults

Habitat Most common in open habitats, rarer in dense forest, but present in all terrestrial habitats; several species often common in gardens and may nest inside greenhouses

Distribution Worldwide except in very cold or dry zones

Mining Bees

A solitary mining bee, *Colletes succinctus*, and her cluster of cells, each with an egg attached to the cell wall. When they hatch, the larvae drop into the liquid mixture of honey and pollen below. Length 0.4 inches (10 mm).

Colletes succinctus

Common name Mining bees

Family Andrenidae

Suborder Apocrita

Order Hymenoptera

Class/Subphylum Insecta/Hexapoda

Number of species About 5,000 (about 1,200 U.S.)

Size From about 0.4 in (10 mm) to about 0.6 in (15 mm)

Key features Mainly hairy bees, mostly dark brown or rusty brown, some black; mainly hairless in subfamily Panurginae; tongue short but pointed at the tip

Habits Both sexes normally found on flowers; they carry nectar and pollen back to the nest on the hind legs; some species are cuckoos in the nests of others

Breeding Females build nests by digging vertical tunnels in the ground, occasionally in dense aggregations with other females; a few species are communal, with several females using parts of a single nest system; males often a different color from females

Diet Adults feed on nectar from many different kinds of flowers; larvae supplied with nectar and pollen, often from only a single species of flower or several closely related species in a single family

Habitat All terrestrial habitats and often among the commonest bees in gardens, especially in springtime; prefer open habitats; common in deserts, rare in dense forest

Distribution Widespread on all continents except Australia and Antarctica

Honeybees and Relatives

The honeybee *Apis mellifera* is found worldwide thanks to commercial beekeeping. It plays an important role in plant reproduction, transferring pollen from plant to plant. Body length (of worker) 0.5 inches (13 mm).

Apis mellifera

Common name Honeybees, stingless bees, bumblebees, orchid bees

Family Apidae

Suborder Apocrita

Order Hymenoptera

Class/Subphylum Insecta/Hexapoda

Number of species About 1,000 (60 U.S.)

Size From about 0.08 in (2 mm) to about 1.1 in (2.7 cm)

Key features Small, hairless, mainly brown or black body (stingless bees); medium-sized, slim-waisted, brown body (honeybees); stout and densely hairy rusty brown or black body, often with red or yellow bands (bumblebees); brilliant metallic-blue or green body, sometimes hairy like bumblebees (orchid bees); tongue long; pollen baskets generally present on hind legs

Habits Most species common on flowers and are important pollinators of many crops; honeybee often domesticated in hives

Breeding Most species often highly social, living in large nests containing thousands of workers (nonbreeding females); social species eventually rear males and females who leave nest for mating purposes; mated queens then found new nest, usually in following spring after winter hibernation; some species are cuckoos in nests of others

Diet Adults feed mainly on nectar; in tropics orchid bees and stingless bees often feed on dung or urine-soaked ground; larvae eat pollen and nectar; larvae of some stingless bees eat carrion

Habitat In all terrestrial habitats from sea level to vegetation limits on mountains; many species common in gardens

Distribution Worldwide in areas that are not too arid or permanently cold; honeybee introduced into the Americas, Australia, and New Zealand

Mayflies

The subimago, or preadult stage, of *Leptophlebia marginata* is known to fly fishermen as the sepia dun. Found across northern and central Europe, it is used as bait to catch trout. Length 0.4 inches (1 cm).

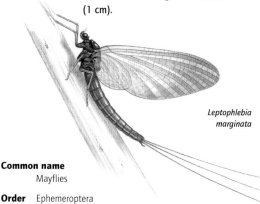

Leptophlebia marginata

Common name
Mayflies

Order Ephemeroptera

Class Insecta

Subphylum Hexapoda

Number of species More than 2,000 (611 U.S.)

Size From about 0.2 in (5 mm) to 1.2 in (3 cm)

Key features Adults with 2 pairs of membranous wings, the first pair much larger than the second, which may be absent altogether in some species; at the end of the abdomen are 3 long "tails" (2 in some families); large compound eyes; antennae short; mouthparts reduced; nymphs have well-developed jaws and also 3 "tails"

Habits Adults spend their short lives on vegetation near water or in courtship swarms; nymphs are usually nocturnal and aquatic, living in all types of fresh water, but not if it is too stagnant; nymphs undergo unique, preadult winged stage (the subimago)

Breeding Usually form mating swarms; males grab females in midair; both males and females usually present, but a few species use parthenogenesis; eggs laid in water

Diet Nymphs mainly vegetarian; adults do not feed

Habitat Ponds, lakes, streams, rivers, and canals; a few species live in brackish water

Distribution Worldwide, especially in temperate zones

Dragonflies and Damselflies

A female southern hawker, *Aeshna cyanea*, lays her eggs in a soft, water-logged tree stump. (*Aeshna* means ugly or misshapen and *cyanea* means dark blue, although there is no blue color present in the female of the species.) The southern hawker is widespread throughout Europe. Wingspan up to 3.5 inches (9 cm) and body length up to 2.8 inches (7 cm).

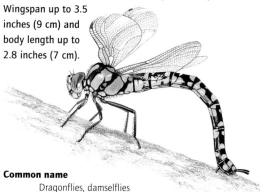

Common name
Dragonflies, damselflies

Order Odonata

Class Insecta

♀ Southern hawker (*Aeshna cyanea*)

Subphylum Hexapoda

Number of species About 6,500 (438 U.S.)

Size From about 0.7 in (19 mm) to 5 in (13 cm)

Key features Head with large compound eyes and well-developed jaws; antennae very short; 2 pairs of transparent wings almost equal in size; abdomen long and slim in most species; dragonflies hold their wings out to the side, damselflies fold their wings over and along the body; jaws in nymphs can be extended for grabbing prey; damselfly nymphs have 3 external gills, dragonfly nymphs have gills inside the rectum

Habits Damselflies normally found hunting for prey close to water; stronger-flying dragonflies may often be found hunting a long way from water; nymphs mostly aquatic

Breeding Males may grab females in midair or pounce on sitting females; some species have complex courtship routines; eggs laid in or near water

Diet Both adults and nymphs are predators

Habitat Any habitat with suitable still or running water, the latter not too fast; some species can inhabit deserts provided water is available at least for a short time

Distribution Found all over the world except for the North and South Poles

Walkingsticks and Leaf Insects

Acrophylla titan, aptly named the titan stick insect or the great brown phasma, is the longest Australian species. The females are generally much larger than the males and are abundant egg layers. Two captive females were observed to lay over 4,000 eggs between them during their lifetime. Body length up to 10 inches (25 cm).

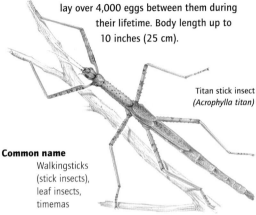

Titan stick insect
(*Acrophylla titan*)

Common name
Walkingsticks (stick insects), leaf insects, timemas

Order Phasmatodea (Phasmida)

Class Insecta

Subphylum Hexapoda

Number of species About 2,500 (32 U.S.)

Size From about 0.5 in (13 mm) to 13 in (33 cm)

Key features Body shape anything from short and broad in leaf insects to very long and thin in walkingsticks; antennae slim, very variable in length; compound eyes fairly small; simple eyes in flying species but often only present in the male; wings (when present) usually only full size in males, many species wingless in both sexes; forewings leathery to protect hind wings; nymphs resemble adults, but are wingless

Habits Almost all species sit around on vegetation and are active at night

Breeding Courtship mainly absent; many males guard the female during egg laying; eggs dropped anywhere or inserted into crevices

Diet All species feed on living vegetation of some kind

Habitat Forests, grassy areas, scrub, semidesert, and desert

Distribution Worldwide, but most common in the tropics; absent from cool, temperate regions

Earwigs

The tawny earwig, *Labidura riparia*, sometimes flies to lights at night and can emit an unpleasant smell when captured. It is found across the southern United States. Length up to 1 inch (2.5 cm).

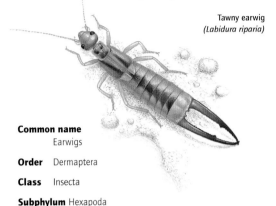

Tawny earwig
(*Labidura riparia*)

Common name
Earwigs

Order Dermaptera

Class Insecta

Subphylum Hexapoda

Number of species About 1,800 (20 U.S.)

Size From about 0.2 in (5 mm) to 1 in (2.5 cm)

Key features Relatively elongate, rather flattened body; head with large or small compound eyes (or lacking eyes) and biting and chewing jaws; winged or wingless; forewings only very small; hind wings semicircular in shape, folding up neatly to fit beneath the forewing covers; cerci highly modified to form "pincers"; nymphs resemble adults

Habits Most are nocturnal; some live in burrows, a few unusual species live on mammals

Breeding Males of some species use the pincers to hold the female; parental care by females not uncommon

Diet Feed as scavengers on a variety of dead and decaying organic matter; some eat flowers; a few are semiparasitic

Habitat Grassland, forests, deserts, and gardens

Distribution Worldwide

Termites

A soldier-caste *Nasutitermes* sp. termite, known as a "nasute" soldier. The species is found in forest undergrowth in lowland areas of Central and South America. Length 0.2 inches (5 mm).

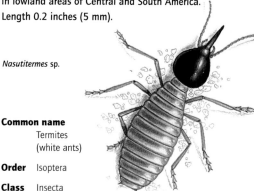

Nasutitermes sp.

Common name
Termites
(white ants)

Order   Isoptera

Class   Insecta

Subphylum Hexapoda

Number of species About 2,300 (44 U.S.)

Size   From about 0.2 in (5 mm) to 1 in (2.5 cm)

Key features Social insects with kings, queens, soldiers, and workers; jaws typically used for biting and chewing; compound eyes (may be reduced or absent); antennae slim and about the same length as the thorax; membranous wings present in sexual forms, absent in workers and soldiers; soldiers often with large jaws or a snoutlike extension of the head; nymphs resemble wingless adults

Habits   Social insects with colonies of up to millions of individuals; live in the ground, often within mounds, or burrow into wood

Breeding Winged sexual forms fly from colonies; females land and release pheromones to attract males; queens lay large numbers of eggs and are fed and looked after by workers

Diet   Fungi and decaying plant material

Habitat Forests, savanna, semidesert, and desert

Distribution Worldwide, but mainly tropical; just a few species in warm, temperate zones

Cockroaches

The American cockroach, *Periplaneta americana*, is also known as the waterbug because of its preference for living in damp places such as water pipes and sewage systems. It is thought to have been introduced to the United States from Africa as early as 1625 and has spread across the world by crawling into grocery packages and being transported to new locations. Body length 1.5–2 inches (3.8–5 cm).

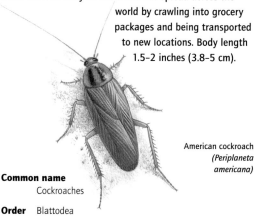

American cockroach
(Periplaneta americana)

Common name
Cockroaches

Order   Blattodea

Class   Insecta

Subphylum Hexapoda

Number of species Around 4,000 (over 50 U.S.)

Size   From about 0.15 in (4 mm) to 4.8 in (12 cm)

Key features Body tends to be rather flattened; head with well-developed compound eyes (except cave dwellers), long, thin antennae with many segments, and chewing mouthparts; pronotum usually forms a shield over the thorax and may extend forward to cover the top of the head; forewings toughened, covering the membranous hind wings; wings may be absent, especially in females; 1 pair of cerci on the end of the abdomen; nymphs resemble wingless adults

Habits   Many species are nocturnal, while some come out in the day and feed from flowers

Breeding Mating may be preceded by courtship; stridulation (hissing) is known to occur in some species; eggs laid in a special purselike structure, the ootheca; parental care is known for a number of species

Diet   Scavengers; many species will eat almost anything edible that they come across

Habitat Grassland, forests, deserts, sand dunes, caves, and human habitations

Distribution Worldwide, but most species found in the tropics

Mantids

Stoneflies

The praying mantis, *Mantis religiosa*, is found waiting for smaller insect prey on flowers and foliage. It was accidentally introduced from southern Europe into the United States in 1899. Length including wings 2.5 inches (6 cm).

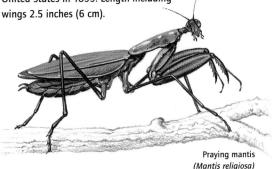

Praying mantis
(*Mantis religiosa*)

The European stonefly, *Perla bipunctata*, is an impressive insect with distinctive yellow markings. It takes three years to mature and up to 30 molts to reach full size. It can be found on rivers and streams, but rarely on ponds. Body length up to 1.6 inches (4 cm).

European stonefly
(*Perla bipunctata*)

Common name Mantids
(praying mantises)

Order Mantodea

Class Insecta

Subphylum Hexapoda

Number of species About 2,000 (20 U.S.)

Size From about 0.4 in (10 mm) to 6 in (15 cm)

Key features Males normally smaller than females; head roughly triangular when seen from front; eyes large and well separated; antennae thin; jaws for cutting and chewing prey; head held well away from the body on elongated first thoracic segment; front legs adapted for grasping prey; forewings leathery, covering membranous hind wings; 1 pair of cerci on the end of the abdomen; nymphs resemble adults or are ant mimics, at least in the early instars

Habits Most species sit on vegetation waiting for prey; some sit on bark, others live on the ground

Breeding Females attract males to them—courtship follows; eggs laid in a special purselike structure, the ootheca; maternal care known in some species

Diet Predators, feeding on other insects and also spiders; occasionally take small vertebrates such as lizards

Habitat Grassland, scrub, forests, semideserts, and deserts

Distribution Mainly tropical in distribution, with a few species in warmer temperate areas

Common name Stoneflies

Order Plecoptera

Class Insecta

Subphylum Hexapoda

Number of species About 2,000 (465 U.S.)

Size From about 0.2 in (5 mm) to 2.5 in (6 cm)

Key features Adults fairly slim bodied, with a cylindrical appearance; head has 2 long, thin antennae and large, bulging compound eyes; chewing mouthparts present but never used; wings membranous, hind wings larger than forewings, wrapped around body and often much longer than the abdomen; some species lack wings, or they may be reduced in size in males; 1 pair of slim cerci, often quite long, on the end of the abdomen; nymphs look like wingless adults but with jaws for feeding; nymphs have gills on the abdomen

Habits Adults always found near water and are often nocturnal; nymphs usually found in well-oxygenated water

Breeding Males and females drum to one another during courtship; eggs laid into water

Diet Some adults do not feed, others eat algae and lichens; nymphs feed either on vegetable matter or more often on other small water creatures

Habitat Fast-flowing rivers and streams and wave-lapped lakesides; just a few species in stiller waters

Distribution Most species found in the cooler, temperate areas of the world

Lice

Lacewings and Relatives

Trichodectes canis, the dog louse, is found all over the world. Large infestations of the parasite can cause considerable irritation to dogs (especially pups), which will try in vain to remove the pests by scratching vigorously. Body length 0.04 inches (1 mm).

Dog louse
(Trichodectes canis)

Common name Lice

Order Phthiraptera

Class Insecta

Subphylum Hexapoda

Number of species About 5,500 (1,000 U.S.)

Size From about 0.02 in (0.5 mm) to 0.4 in (10 mm)

Key features Flattened, wingless insects; antennae short; eyes small or absent; mouthparts used for chewing in 2 suborders and for sucking in the 3rd suborder; legs with strong claws on the foot to grasp the hair or feathers of host mammals and birds; nymphs are like tiny pale adults

Habits Live on or near their host birds or mammals, which include humans

Breeding Eggs are attached to the hair or feathers of host animals

Diet Feed either on bird feathers or mammal skin, or suck blood

Habitat Found wherever their hosts are, as well as terrestrial mammals and birds; hosts also include seals, penguins, and oceanic birds that only come to land to breed

Distribution Worldwide

Libelloides coccajus is a distinctive lacewing. It looks like a small dragonfly, with long antennae and yellow-and-black wings. The species, found mainly in Europe, is highly predatory on other insects. Body length 0.75 inches (18 mm).

Libelloides coccajus

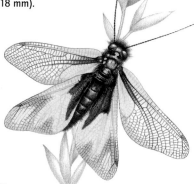

Common name Lacewings, mantid flies, ant lions, owlflies, butterfly lions

Order Neuroptera

Class Insecta

Subphylum Hexapoda

Number of species About 4,500 (285 U.S.)

Size From about 0.2 in (5 mm) to 1.8 in (4.6 cm)

Key features Adult head has longish, slim antennae, sometimes with knobs at the end; compound eyes vary from small to very large in relation to size of head; chewing jaws present; both pairs of wings membranous and held tentlike over abdomen; larvae usually with large mandibles, sometimes covered in detritus; pupa usually encased in a silk cocoon

Habits Many are nocturnal; virtually all have a weak, rather flappy flight; some day fliers may be mistaken for butterflies; larvae found on all sorts of vegetation, including bark, and on or in the ground

Breeding Courtship can be quite complex; eggs, which may be on long stalks of hardened mucus, laid on vegetation

Diet Adults predaceous, but some also take pollen and nectar; larvae predaceous

Habitat Forests, orchards, savanna, grassland, sand dunes, semidesert, and desert

Distribution Worldwide

Caddisflies

An adult of the great red sedge, *Phryganea grandis*, a European species found as far north as Lapland. The larvae build their protective cases with plant material arranged in a spiral. Body length 0.5 inches (13 mm).

Great red sedge
(*Phryganea grandis*)

Common name Caddisflies

Order Trichoptera

Class Insecta

Subphylum Hexapoda

Number of species About 7,000 (1,262 U.S.)

Size From about 0.06 in (1.5 mm) to 1 in (2.5 cm)

Key features Adults mothlike, with a slender, elongate body; most species drably colored in all shades of brown to black, a few brightly colored; body and wings hairy; wings held tentlike over the body; head bears threadlike antennae that can be 2 or 3 times the body length; large compound eyes used in locating each other; mouthparts reduced or almost nonexistent; most larvae similar to caterpillars, living in cases or silken tubes; some free-living, without a case

Habits Adults often nocturnal, usually found on vegetation near water; most larvae aquatic, living in water of all kinds

Breeding Males often form huge mating swarms over or near water; eggs laid in, near, or under water

Diet Adults either do not feed or just take liquid food; larvae may be vegetarian or predaceous

Habitat Lakes, ponds, streams, and rivers

Distribution Worldwide

Fleas

The dog flea, *Ctenocephalides canis*, and the cat flea, *Ctenocephalides felis*, are probably the most common domestic fleas, with a worldwide distribution. The flea life cycle takes about three weeks, but eggs can remain dormant for long periods in cool weather. Length 0.1 inches (3–4 mm).

Dog flea
(*Ctenocephalides canis*)

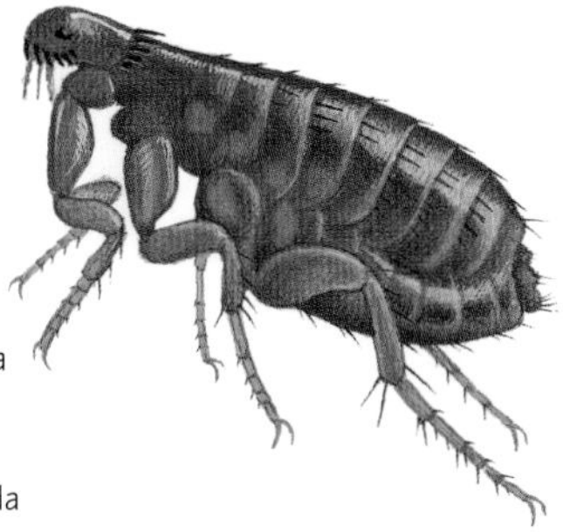

Common name Fleas

Order Siphonaptera

Class Insecta

Subphylum Hexapoda

Number of species About 2,380 (325 U.S.)

Size From about 0.04 in (1 mm) to 0.5 in (13 mm)

Key features Adults very flattened from side to side; wingless; hind legs modified for jumping; head without compound eyes; simple eyes may be absent or well developed; mouthparts adapted for sucking blood

Habits Adults live on their hosts; hosts are mainly mammals, but also a few birds; larvae live in nests or close to where the hosts live

Breeding Breeding cycle of fleas often linked to that of the host; eggs normally laid in the host's nest or living area

Diet Blood for the adults, shed skin and other edible bits and pieces for the larvae

Habitat Wherever the hosts are found

Distribution Worldwide

Centipedes

Millipedes

Scutigera coleoptrata, the house centipede, is a species from Europe, but now has been introduced and is widespread in the United States and Mexico. It lives indoors and outdoors, but is the only centipede that can reproduce indoors. It preys on other insects and, with its 15 pairs of legs, is an extremely fast runner. Body length up to 1.5 inches (3.8 cm).

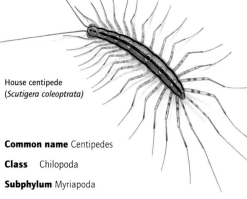

House centipede
(*Scutigera coleoptrata*)

Common name Centipedes

Class Chilopoda

Subphylum Myriapoda

Number of species About 2,500 (not known U.S)

Size From about 0.4 in (10 mm) to 10 in (25 cm)

Key features Body formed from head and multisegmented trunk; each trunk segment (except the first and last 2) has a pair of legs; appendages on first trunk segment modified to inject poison into prey; head has a pair of slim antennae and chewing mouthparts (1 pair of mandibles and 2 pairs of maxillae); eyes, when present, simple or compound

Habits Mainly nocturnal, when they can be found moving around the habitat they live in looking for prey; 1 family lives in the soil, moving around in worm burrows and natural cracks

Breeding Courtship described for some species; otherwise males leave spermatophores lying around for females to collect; female parental care is known in some species

Diet Mainly carnivorous, but some soil dwellers feed on vegetable matter

Habitat Grassland, forests, semideserts, and deserts

Distribution Worldwide

A giant millipede, order Spirostreptida, curled up in a defensive coil. The Spirostreptida are subtropical and tropical millipedes. Length 0.5 inches (13 cm) to 11 inches (28 cm).

Giant millipede
(order Spirostreptida)

Common name Millipedes

Class Diplopoda

Subphylum Myriapoda

Number of species About 10,000 (2,167 U.S.)

Size From about 0.16 in (4 mm) to 12 in (30 cm)

Key features Head with 1 pair of very short antennae, 1 pair of eyes, and chewing mouthparts; body shape very variable, from long and cylindrical to short and humped or long and flattened; all have many segments with 2 pairs of legs per segment; some species can roll up into a ball when threatened

Breeding Courtship rituals are quite common; some males use sound communication to attract the female; female usually makes some form of nest in which eggs are laid and then left

Diet Plant material, especially if it is dead and decaying

Habitat Forests, grassland, desert and semidesert, mountains, and gardens

Distribution Worldwide, but commoner in tropical regions

Water Fleas and Fairy Shrimps

The powerful second antennae of the *Daphnia* water flea make jerking downstrokes that propel the tiny animal up through the water. Five eggs can be seen clearly in the brood pouch of this female. Length up to 0.1 inches (3 mm).

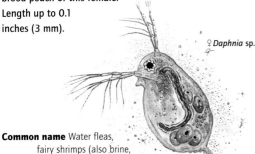

♀ *Daphnia* sp.

Common name Water fleas, fairy shrimps (also brine, clam, and tadpole shrimps)

Class Branchiopoda

Subphylum Crustacea

Number of species About 800 species representing 23 families in 3 orders

Size 0.01 in (0.3 mm) to 4 in (10 cm)

Key features A diverse group characterized by paddlelike appendages on segmented trunk, with gills growing from leg bases; first antennae and second maxillae are vestigial; abdomen has paired "tails" called cercopods; carapace may or may not be present

Habits Swim using antennae or trunk appendages, or crawl on surface; often phototactic (attracted to light); populations often cyclical, with peaks in warm, wet seasons

Breeding Most species reproduce parthenogenetically, with males only appearing when population is under stress; females produce 2 kinds of eggs—summer eggs develop immediately, winter (resistant) eggs may lie dormant for many years

Diet Mostly suspension feeders on bacteria, algae, and detritus; occasionally feed on multicellular plant material and carrion; some water fleas are predatory

Habitat Mostly in temporary fresh water such as puddles, dew ponds, and seasonal lakes; water fleas live in permanent streams and lakes; some water fleas and brine shrimps are adapted to brackish and salty water

Distribution Worldwide

Barnacles

The acorn barnacle, *Semibalanus balanoides*—a European species—grows on rocks on the middle and lower shore. Its shape varies according to habitat, growing more columnar in crowded populations. Diameter about 0.4 inches (10 mm).

Acorn barnacle (*Semibalanus balanoides*)

Common name Barnacles

Infraclass Cirripedia

Class Maxillopoda

Subphylum Crustacea

Number of species About 900 species representing 56 families in 6 orders

Size From a fraction of an inch to 10 in (25 cm) tall and 3 in (8 cm) in diameter

Key features Body form variable; sessile species protected by fortress of heavily calcified plates; curly thoracic feeding legs can be extended through "hatch doors"

Habits True barnacles are sessile as adults; smaller orders contain rock-boring and parasitic forms

Breeding Sessile barnacles are hermaphrodites and reproduce with close neighbors; larvae pass through 6 nauplius stages and 1 cyprid settlement stage before metamorphosing into adults; life span can be up to 10 years

Diet Sessile species are omnivorous suspension feeders, eating all manner of detritus; parasites feed on tissues and body fluids of host

Habitat Marine, from high tide mark on rocky shores to deepest ocean trenches

Distribution Found in all oceans and adjoining seas

Mantis Shrimps

Isopods

Mantis shrimps of the genus *Squilla* are tropical and often brightly colored. Their awesome weaponry means they have little to fear from any other animal and no need for camouflage. Length 12 inches (30 cm).

Squilla sp.

Common name Mantis shrimps

Order Stomatopoda

Class Malacostraca

Subphylum Crustacea

Number of species About 400 species representing 17 families

Size From 2 in (5 cm) to 16 in (40 cm)

Key features Robust, often slightly flattened body; carapace small, only covering front half of thorax; second pair of thoracic legs modified into huge barbed, powerful, clawlike subchelae used for hunting; last 3 pairs of thoracic legs slender and stiltlike, used along with tail to support body off the sea floor

Habits Aggressive and bold; adults bottom dwelling, may burrow in mud or other soft substrate, or occupy dens in rocks and coral; larvae swim freely in open water

Breeding Male and female pairs come together for courtship and mating; female tends eggs and young larvae alone in a den

Diet Exclusively carnivorous and predaceous; prey includes mollusks, fish, worms, and other crustaceans, such as small crabs and shrimps

Habitat Exclusively marine, in warm intertidal and subtidal waters surrounding most tropical coastlines; usually in less than 65 feet (20 m) of water

Distribution Mainly in tropical and warm temperate zones of Atlantic, Pacific, and Indian Oceans, and adjoining seas; a few species live in cool temperate zones

The sea slater *Ligia oceanica* is found in large numbers above the high-water mark on rocky coasts around Europe. It emerges at dusk and can often be seen scuttling over damp rock surfaces. This species is also known as the sea roach and occurs in North America from Maine to Cape Cod. Length up to 1.2 inches (3 cm).

Ligia oceanica

Common name Sea slaters (sea roaches, gribbles), woodlice, and pill bugs (sow bugs)

Order Isopoda

Class Malacostraca

Subphylum Crustacea

Number of species About 10,000 species representing 120 families and 9 suborders

Size Most 0.2 in (5 mm) to 0.6 in (15 mm), but can reach up to 16.5 in (42 cm)

Key features Segmented body with dorsal plates capable of overlapping to some extent; 7 pairs of walking legs; delicate abdominal appendages, used for swimming and respiration, are enclosed in land-dwelling species

Habits Bottom-dwelling crawlers; most can also swim; many burrow; some bore into wood

Breeding Mate after partial molt; females brood eggs and larvae in special chamber; young released at late manca stage or as miniature adults

Diet Mostly omnivorous scavengers and deposit feeders; some species specialize in grazing algae; woodlice eat rotting wood; a few large marine species are active predators of small invertebrates, and some families have blood-sucking parasitic representatives

Habitat Mostly marine, from tidal and estuarine zones to deep sea; also in fresh water and on land (pill bugs and woodlice)

Distribution Worldwide

Shrimps and Prawns

The common or brown shrimp, *Crangon crangon*, is an important commercial species found in the northeastern Atlantic and the Mediterranean. Length up to 4 inches (10 cm). The northern shrimp, *Pandalus borealis*, occurs in the North Atlantic, the North Pacific, and the Arctic oceans. It is a long-lived species, with a life span of up to 8 years. Length up to 6.5 inches (16.5 cm).

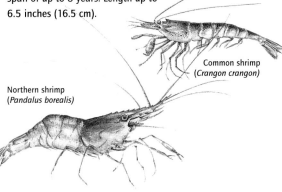

Common shrimp
(*Crangon crangon*)

Northern shrimp
(*Pandalus borealis*)

Common name Shrimps, prawns

Infraorders Penaeidea, Caridea, and Stenopodidea (Natantia)

Order Decapoda

Class/Subphylum Malacostraca/Crustacea

Number of species About 3,000 species, representing 3 infraorders and 2 suborders

Size Most less than 2 in (5 cm), but up to 14 in (36 cm) long

Key features Head and thorax protected by cylindrical carapace; head bears long first antennae, second antennae also have leaf-shaped scale; thorax bears 5 pairs of walking legs, abdomen has segmental swimming legs and tail fan

Habits Live in the open sea or near, or on the bottom of, the seabed; may form large swarms; many species migrate vertically each day to feed near surface at night

Breeding Males and females exist in most species, with female carrying eggs until hatching; some species are hermaphroditic; planktonic zoea larvae develop into postlarvae with full set of appendages, which in turn molt to become adults

Diet Scavenging omnivores

Habitat Aquatic, in marine, brackish, as well as freshwater environments

Distribution Worldwide

Lobsters and Crayfish

The European or common lobster, *Homarus gammarus*, is highly valued as seafood and rarely achieves its potential life span of 15-20 years before being caught by fishermen. The lobsters live in holes in rocks or tunnels beneath the sand and are found from the lower shore to a depth of about 200 feet (60 m) Length 18 inches (46 cm).

European lobster
(*Homarus gammarus*)

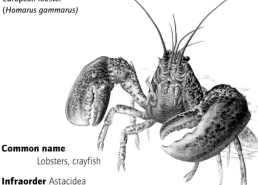

Common name Lobsters, crayfish

Infraorder Astacidea

Order Decapoda

Class/Subphylum Malacostraca/Crustacea

Number of species Many hundreds in total, representing 7 living families

Size Usually up to 24 in (60 cm) long; occasionally 4.2 ft (1.3 m); the largest lobsters weigh over 44 lb (20 kg)

Key features Robust body with cylindrical carapace; abdomen long, slightly flattened, and segmented; first walking legs modified into large pincers (chelipeds); first antennae have two branches (biramous); second antennae shorter and lack antennal scales

Habits Nocturnal, solitary, and aggressive; several marine species migrate inshore to breed

Breeding Mating occurs after last molt; female broods eggs on abdominal pleopods; larvae are planktonic and settle as miniature adults

Diet Scavenging omnivores; nonpredaceous, but will grab anything that passes by; crayfish may also filter feed

Habitat Aquatic bottom dwellers; lobsters are marine, crayfish live in freshwater habitats

Distribution Worldwide

Hermit Crabs

True Crabs

Pagurus bernhardus occupies the disused shell of the gastropod *Buccinum undatum*. *Pagurus bernhardus* is the largest and most common of the northwestern European hermit crabs, occurring on all British coasts as well as south to the Atlantic coast of Portugal and north to Norway. Length 1.4 inches (3.5 cm).

The shore crab, *Carcinus maenas*, is common in shallow water. It is a native of Europe, but has now spread throughout the world. Length 1.6 inches (4 cm).

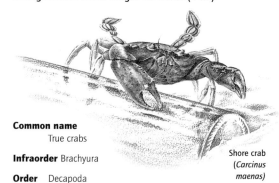

Shore crab
(*Carcinus maenas*)

Pagurus bernhardus

Common name Hermit crabs

Superfamily Paguroidea

Infraorder Anomura

Order Decapoda

Class/Subphylum Malacostraca/Crustacea

Number of species Several hundred species in 6 families

Size Most no longer than 6 in (15 cm); shell-less relatives may have carapace of up to 12 in (30 cm)

Key features Small, crablike animal; 4th and 5th pair of walking legs reduced; soft, twisted abdomen usually carried in gastropod shell; 1st legs modified into large chelipeds; 2nd and 3rd pairs used for walking; 4th pair used for grasping shell house from within

Habits Solitary and active; growing individuals upgrade to larger shells; fights over shells are common

Breeding Mating occurs out of shells immediately following female molt; eggs carried on abdomen inside shell and released as planktonic zoea larvae; larvae molt through several stages; when adult form is reached, they seek a shell in which to live

Diet Omnivorous scavengers and filter feeders

Habitat Mostly marine, from deep oceans to intertidal zones; some spend long periods out of water

Distribution Found in all the world's oceans and on land close to the sea throughout tropical zones

Common name True crabs

Infraorder Brachyura

Order Decapoda

Class/Subphylum Malacostraca/Crustacea

Number of species About 6,000 species representing 71 families

Size Carapace 0.1 in (2.5 mm) to 15 in (38 cm), leg span up to 13 ft (4 m)

Key features Short body with reduced abdomen tucked underneath flattened carapace; 4 pairs of walking legs, plus 1 pair of large claws

Habits Very varied; mostly nocturnal; may be solitary or gregarious; mostly aquatic and benthic (bottom dwelling); some swim well, others adapted to life on land

Breeding Mating occurs postmolt; females brood eggs under body attached to reduced abdomen; larvae pass through several zoeal stages and settle as postlarval megalops; a few land crabs skip the larval stage and develop directly into tiny adults

Diet Omnivorous scavengers of plant and animal material, filter feeders, and active predators of aquatic and terrestrial invertebrates, fish, and other animals

Habitat Marine, freshwater, and terrestrial habitats, including beaches, shallow and deep oceans, mangroves, coral reefs, rivers, lakes, estuaries, grassland, and forests

Distribution Worldwide

Horseshoe Crabs

Scorpions

The horseshoe crab *Limulus polyphemus* lives in water up to 75 feet (23 m) deep from the Gulf of Maine to the Gulf of Mexico. It spawns on shore in spring, and the eggs take a few weeks to hatch. The young are miniature replicas of the adults with a batonlike tail. Body length up to 24 inches (61 cm).

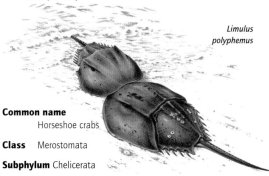

Limulus polyphemus

Common name
Horseshoe crabs

Class   Merostomata

Subphylum Chelicerata

Number of species 4 (1 U.S.)

Size   From about 2 in (5 cm) to about 24 in (60 cm)

Key features Body short and broad, tapering toward the rear, dull gray; divided into 2 parts: a forward part (prosoma or cephalothorax) and rear part (opisthosoma or abdomen); large shell-like shield covering the cephalothorax, which has a compound eye on either side, plus 2 pairs of smaller, simple eyes (median and lateral); 6 pairs of appendages; body terminated by long spine called a telson

Habits   Sea living, foraging for food on the bottom mud and ooze

Breeding Millions of individuals migrate to the seashore in a mass orgy of egg laying

Diet   Small invertebrates such as mollusks, crustaceans, and worms

Habitat Open sea, except when breeding

Distribution Seas around North America and Asia

One of the largest scorpions found in Africa, the African emperor scorpion, *Pandinus imperator*, does not use its stinger to kill prey, but as a last resort in defense. Body length up to 4 inches (10 cm).

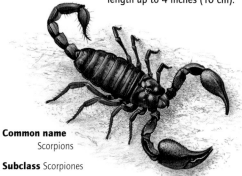

Common name
Scorpions

Subclass Scorpiones

Class   Arachnida

Subphylum Chelicerata

African emperor scorpion
(*Pandinus imperator*)

Number of species About 1,500 (about 75 U.S.)

Size   From about 1.6 in (4 cm) to about 8 in (20 cm)

Key features Body flattened, mostly brown, black, or yellowish, sometimes deep green; body broad at the front, tapering backward to a long, upwardly curved flexible tail bearing a hinged stinger at its tip; pedipalps modified into 2 large pincerlike claws; a pair of comblike structures (pectines) trails down between the last pair of legs; eyes tiny, 2 in the center of the cephalothorax, 2–5 more on each side; breathing via book lungs

Habits   Mostly nocturnal, spending the day hidden in crevices, under stones or bark, or in burrows up to about 39 in (100 cm) deep; all species hunt other small animals; some species wander in search of prey, others sit and wait in ambush

Breeding Courtship is complex and consists of a "dance" performed by male and female; females give birth to live young, which assemble on their mother's back and are carried around for some time; some species are parthenogenetic and produce young without first mating

Diet   Insects, other arachnids (especially scorpions), centipedes, millipedes, snails, frogs, toads, lizards, small snakes, birds, and small rodents

Habitat Most common in deserts; also present in mountains, rain forests, gardens, in and around buildings, and on the seashore; a few blind species in caves

Distribution Worldwide, but mainly found in warmer tropical areas; only 1 species as far north as Alberta in North America; absent from northern Europe except as an accidental introduction in buildings

Mites and Ticks

As its common name suggests, the hedgehog tick, *Ixodes hexagonus* from Europe, is numerous on hedgehogs. A heavy infestation, particularly on young hedgehogs, can cause problems. Body length up to 0.3 inches (7 mm).

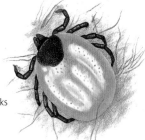

Hedgehog tick (*Ixodes hexagonus*)

Common name
Mites and ticks

Subclass Acari

Class Arachnida

Subphylum Chelicerata

Number of species About 45,000 (8,000+ U.S.)

Size Body length from about 0.003 in (0.08 mm) to about 0.6 in (15 mm)

Key features Body mainly black or brown, but many species red, green, or yellow; no division into cephalothorax and abdomen; pedipalps small, simple, and leglike; usually 4 pairs of walking legs; no tail or other appendages on abdomen; larvae have only 6 legs

Habits Many mites are free living in soil, on plants, or in both fresh and salt water; others develop within plants or on the bodies of animals; all ticks are parasitic on mammals, birds, and reptiles

Breeding Males may fight over access to females; sperm is transferred to the females by both direct and indirect methods; eggs hatch as 6-legged larvae, which molt to become 8-legged nymphs; females of many ticks lay several thousand eggs; ticks may need to use more than 1 kind of host in order to complete their life cycle

Diet Mites feed on all kinds of vegetable and animal materials; gall-forming mites are often restricted to a single genus or species of host plant; many mites take solid food; all ticks feed on blood

Habitat In soil, on plants, and on living animals in every conceivable type of habitat

Distribution Worldwide, including the deep seas and the polar regions; mites are probably the most ubiquitous of all animals

Tarantulas

The Mexican red knee tarantula, *Brachypelma smithi*, is found in the Pacific Coast regions of Mexico. Body length up to 2.4 inches (6 cm).

Mexican red-knee tarantula (*Brachypelma smithi*)

Common name Tarantulas (bird-eating spiders, baboon spiders, whistling spiders)

Family Theraphosidae

Suborder Mygalomorphae

Order Araneae

Subclass Aranae

Class Arachnida

Subphylum Chelicerata

Number of species About 1,000 (about 30 U.S.)

Size Body length from about 1 in (2.5 cm) to 5 in (13 cm)

Key features Large, abundantly hairy body; usually blackish or brownish, but sometimes bluish or purplish or boldly marked with orange, yellow, or white; 8 very small eyes forming a close group; legs thick and hairy, each with 2 claws at the tip and a tuft of hair on the underside; males longer legged than females and sometimes with brighter colors

Habits Active at night, spending the day in burrows or in cavities in trees; hunting performed by touch and via sensory hairs; no web built; eyesight poor

Breeding Males wander at night in search of females in their burrows; mating is brief, lasting only a minute or so; females not usually aggressive toward males; eggs laid in burrow or other cavity, sometimes carried around by the female; females are long-lived (20 years or more) and produce many broods

Diet Mainly insects; also spiders, millipedes, sow bugs (woodlice), frogs, toads, lizards, small snakes (including rattlesnakes), and occasionally small birds or mice; long periods without food are not harmful

Habitat Deserts, savannas, and forests, mainly at low elevations; often in houses in the tropics

Distribution Mainly in warm areas; absent from Europe; U.S. species mostly in the southwestern deserts, absent from the southeastern U.S.

Funnel-Web Spiders

The Sydney funnel-web spider, *Atrax robustus*, the most deadly spider in the world, burrows beneath logs and stones in cool places in eastern Australia. Body length up to 1.5 inches (4 cm).

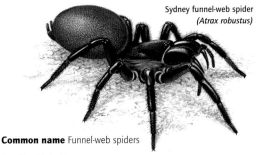

Sydney funnel-web spider
(Atrax robustus)

Common name Funnel-web spiders

Family Dipluridae

Suborder Mygalomorphae

Order Araneae

Subclass Aranae

Class Arachnida

Subphylum Chelicerata

Number of species About 250 (about 10 U.S.)

Size Body length from about 0.1 in (3 mm) to about 2 in (5 cm)

Key features Easily recognized by the long, widely separated spinnerets, which can be half the length of the abdomen or more; body mainly brown or black, rather long and flat; 8 small eyes grouped closely together on a slightly raised tubercle

Habits Web a broad, rather untidy sheet of dense, clothlike silk, often with a bluish tinge; usually placed among tree roots, in crevices in fallen trees, or among rocks; the spider waits in a tube set to one side of the web; some species can be aggressive and dangerous

Breeding Males (which are only slightly smaller than females) leave their webs and wander in search of females at night; female usually lays eggs within the web's retreat, but in some species she carries them around with her

Diet Insects, spiders, millipedes, worms, woodlice (sow bugs), and snails; larger funnel-web spiders can tackle frogs and lizards

Habitat Woodlands, mainly among the mossy base of trees, but also among rocks or on tree trunks; some species found in gardens; several eyeless species live in caves

Distribution Mainly tropical and subtropical, but a few species in southern Europe (Spain) and North America

Net-Casting Spiders

Deinopis guatemalensis, a tropical species, hangs above its insect prey, preparing to drop its net over an unsuspecting bug. Body length up to 0.8 inches (20 mm).

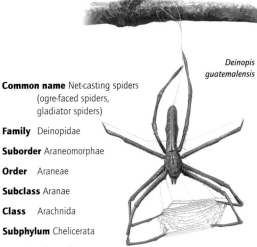

*Deinopis
guatemalensis*

Common name Net-casting spiders (ogre-faced spiders, gladiator spiders)

Family Deinopidae

Suborder Araneomorphae

Order Araneae

Subclass Aranae

Class Arachnida

Subphylum Chelicerata

Number of species About 60 (1 U.S.)

Size Body length 0.5 in (13 mm) to 1.2 in (3 cm)

Key features Body long, slim, and twiglike, usually light brown; in *Deinopis* the small, flat face is almost entirely occupied by 2 huge staring eyes, below which are 2 tiny eyes (plus 4 more on top of the carapace, making 8 in all); in *Menneus* all the eyes are small

Habits Active at night, holding a tiny web in their front legs; the web is thrown over prey as it passes; during the day the spiders resemble twigs

Breeding Males are slightly smaller and more slender than females, with extremely long legs; female *Deinopis* constructs a globular egg sac suspended on a long silken line beneath a leaf; the finished sac is camouflaged with bits of leaf

Diet Various insects

Habitat On low trees and bushes in woods, rain forests, grasslands, and gardens; often common in built-up areas, sometimes on walls and fences

Distribution Mainly in warm areas, especially Australia; only a single species in North America (Florida); none in Europe

Crab Spiders

Lynx Spiders

The common flower spider, *Misumena vatia*, awaits prey on a daisy. It is also found on goldenrod and other white or yellow flowers, giving it the alternative common name of goldenrod spider. Body length up to 0.4 inches (10 mm).

Oxyopes heterophthalmus is found on low vegetation such as heather, where it lies in wait or chases prey. It is widespread in France, the Netherlands, and southern Europe. Body length up to 0.3 inches (8 mm).

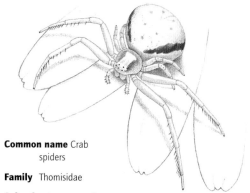

♀ Common flower spider or goldenrod spider (*Misumena vatia*)

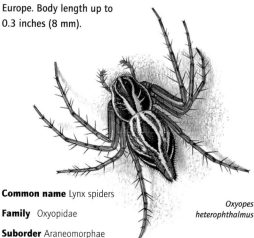

Oxyopes heterophthalmus

Common name Crab spiders

Family Thomisidae

Suborder Araneomorphae

Order Araneae

Subclass Aranae

Class Arachnida

Subphylum Chelicerata

Number of species More than 2,000 (about 250 U.S.)

Size Body length from about 0.08 in (2 mm) to about 0.8 in (20 mm)

Key features Eight eyes, often on raised humps in 2 backwardly curving rows of 4 eyes each; body usually short and broad (but can be long and thin); back two pairs of legs often short and rather stumpy; front two pairs usually much longer and slimmer; each tarsus bears 2 claws; chelicerae lack teeth; venom usually very powerful

Habits Found on the ground, on leaves, or on flowers, usually remaining still for long periods in an ambush position; no silken webs built for catching prey; 1 species partially social

Breeding Males usually much smaller than females and normally a different color; mating generally takes place without any preceding courtship; during mating the male hangs upside down beneath the female, clinging to the underside of her abdomen; she may catch prey and feed while the male is thus occupied; females stand guard over their egg sacs, but often die before the babies hatch

Diet Most kinds of insects or other spiders

Habitat Almost anywhere: forests, grasslands, deserts, mountains, beaches, gardens, and houses

Distribution Worldwide, except the very driest and coldest areas

Common name Lynx spiders

Family Oxyopidae

Suborder Araneomorphae

Order Araneae

Subclass Aranae

Class Arachnida

Subphylum Chelicerata

Number of species About 500 (about 15 U.S.)

Size Body length from about 0.1 in (3 mm) to about 0.7 in (18 mm)

Key features Body mainly brown or green; cephalothorax high and oval; abdomen tapers off to a point; 8 eyes, of which 6 are arranged in hexagonal pattern with 2 smaller eyes below; legs distinctive, covered with numerous long spines that stand out at right angles

Habits Sit-and-wait or pursuit predators found mainly on vegetation; agile enough to leap up and catch insects in flight; use neither a web nor retreat except in *Tapinillus*

Breeding In most species mating is preceded by simple courtship; mating may take place suspended from a silken dragline; in 1 species male also wraps female in bridal veil; females sit and guard their egg sacs

Diet Insects; spiders, including members of own species

Habitat Mainly open places, meadows, savanna, desert, ' edges, a few species in forest

Distribution About 95% of species found in the tropi also U.S. and Europe

Sheet-Web Weavers

Agelena labyrinthica, the grass funnel weaver, can be found among low vegetation and makes a sheet web with a tubular retreat. Body length up to 0.6 inches (15 mm).

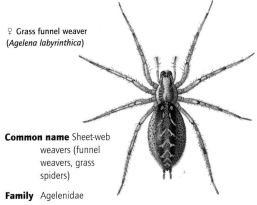

♀ Grass funnel weaver
(*Agelena labyrinthica*)

Common name Sheet-web weavers (funnel weavers, grass spiders)

Family Agelenidae

Suborder Araneomorphae

Order Araneae

Subclass Aranae

Class Arachnida

Subphylum Chelicerata

Number of species About 800 (over 300 U.S.)

Size From about 0.08 in (2 mm) to about 0.8 in (20 mm)

Key features Longish, densely hairy, brown or blackish-brown body carried on long legs that are abundantly spiny and hairy; usually 8 eyes in 2 horizontal rows; some cave species eyeless; a pair of peglike spinnerets protrudes from abdomen tip and so is visible from above

Habits All species build a broad sheet web with a funnel at one side; shady corners and hollows are often favored sites; prey will be attacked both by day and after dark; some of the larger species often wander around houses at night; 2 species are social

Breeding Males and females about equal in size; males enter females' webs and announce their presence by tapping on the silk; in some species males and females cohabit for long periods in the female's web; eggs are laid beneath bark or stones, or within an exposed silken nest

Diet Insects of all types

Habitat Houses, cellars, barns, outhouses, mountains, woods, meadows, marshes, and roadsides; in dark corners or on low bushes and among grass or rocks

Distribution Worldwide but usually avoiding very dry areas and absent from the coldest zones; more common in temperate regions than in the tropics

Orb Weavers

Females of the wasp spider, *Argiope bruennichi*, have a quite unmistakable appearance, being large and strikingly colored. They build their extensive orb webs near ground level. Body length up to 0.9 inches (23 mm).

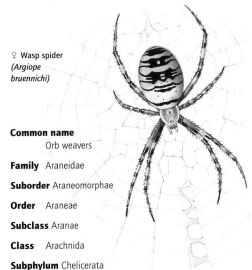

♀ Wasp spider
(*Argiope bruennichi*)

Common name Orb weavers

Family Araneidae

Suborder Araneomorphae

Order Araneae

Subclass Aranae

Class Arachnida

Subphylum Chelicerata

Number of species About 5,000 (about 200 U.S.)

Size Body length from about 0.08 in (2 mm) to about 1.8 in (4.5 cm)

Key features Body shape and color incredibly varied; can be smooth or spiny, oval or elongate, flattened or spherical, brown or brightly colored; 8 small eyes arranged in 2 horizontal rows of 4; third pair of legs always the shortest

Habits Most species build an orb web and sit in the center or in a retreat to one side; webs usually sited in low vegetation, sometimes in trees; webs sometimes communal; some species build a reduced web, swing a prey-catching "bola" (a line weighted with a sticky blob of silk), or have no web at all and catch prey by sitting in wait like crab spiders

Breeding Males generally smaller than females, sometimes very much so; courtship usually consists of male vibrating threads of female's web; no courtship in some species with very small males; egg sacs usually placed among leaves or other vegetation, sometimes large and suspended like fruit

Diet Insects of all kinds

Habitat In every kind of terrestrial habitat; some species live in caves

Distribution Worldwide in habitable regions

Limpets and Top Shells

Whelks and Cone Shells

Patella vulgata, the common limpet, is slow growing and can live for 15 years. It is found from northern Norway to the Mediterranean Sea. Length 2.4 inches (6 cm).

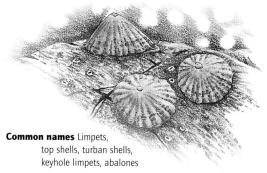

Common names Limpets, top shells, turban shells, keyhole limpets, abalones

Common limpet
(*Patella vulgata*)

Order Archaeogastropoda

Subclass Prosobranchia

Class Gastropoda

Phylum Mollusca

Number of species Unknown

Size 0.08 in (2 mm) to about 16 in (40 cm)

Key features Adult body usually asymmetrical and spiral (not obviously so in abalones and limpets); head normally with 1 or 2 pairs of sensory tentacles, usually with eyes, statocyst, mouth, and radula; well-developed creeping foot with sole; during development body organs and mantle may undergo torsion; bearing 1 flattened shell with apertures arranged in a row (abalones), a cone-shaped shell (limpets), or a spiral shell (top shells, etc.); shell usually lined with mother-of-pearl; head, body, and foot may be withdrawn into shell or covered by it; in top shells shell may be closed by an operculum; no operculum in abalones and limpets; 2 nephridia (excretory organs); well-developed mantle cavity housing ctenidia (gills) and osphradium (organ of scent detection) in some marine species

Habits Adults bottom-dwelling marine or freshwater animals; found in all depths in aquatic environments; foot used for creeping

Breeding Sexes separate; copulation may occur; fertilized egg develops into microscopic planktonic larva in marine forms

Diet Generally herbivores

Habitat Almost all marine, generally living on rocks, reefs, or other hard surfaces

Distribution All the world's seas and oceans; most common between the tidemarks and in shallow water

Nucella lapillus, a dog whelk, is found on rocky shores in northwestern Europe. Height 1.2 inches (3 cm). The waved whelk, *Buccinum undatum*, is often found in waters of the eastern United States and Europe. Height 3 inches (8 cm).

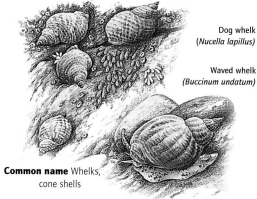

Dog whelk
(*Nucella lapillus*)

Waved whelk
(*Buccinum undatum*)

Common name Whelks, cone shells

Order Neogastropoda

Subclass Prosobranchia

Class Gastropoda

Phylum Mollusca

Number of species Unknown

Size 0.04 in (1 mm) to 18 in (45 cm)

Key features Adult body usually asymmetrical with a spiral, coiled shell; head quite well developed, with 1 or 2 pairs of sensory tentacles, usually with eyes, statocyst, mouth, and radula; well-developed creeping foot with sole; during development and growth the body organs and mantle covering them may rotate between 90 and 180 degrees in relation to the foot (known as torsion); head, body, and foot may be withdrawn into shell or at least covered by it; shell may be closed by a horny stopper (the operculum) attached to tail of foot; body has 2 nephridia (excretory organs), a well-developed mantle cavity housing ctenidia (gills), and an osphradium (organ of scent detection)

Habits Adults mainly bottom-dwelling marine animals; locomotion is by creeping foot

Breeding Sexes separate; mating may occur; fertilized egg develops into microscopic planktonic larva in most marine forms

Diet Generally carnivores, preying on various invertebrates; some cone shells can catch fish

Habitat Almost all marine, generally living on rocks, reefs, or other hard surfaces

Distribution All the world's seas and oceans

Sea Slugs

Snails and Slugs

The sea lemon, *Archidoris pseudoargus*, is commonly found on northwestern European shores. It is a large, warty slug and feeds mainly on sponges. Size up to 5 inches (13 cm).

Common name Sea slugs

Order Nudibranchia

Subclass Opisthobranchia

Class Gastropoda

Phylum Mollusca

Number of species About 1,700

Size 0.04 in (1 mm) to 8 in (20 cm)

Key features Adult body sluglike; uncoiled and lacking a shell and operculum, although often bearing exposed tentaclelike structures; body may be narrow or broad, with well-developed, adhesive, solelike foot on the underside, often ornamented by gills and papillae; head bears 1 or 2 pairs of sensory tentacles arranged in various ways; no mantle cavity; there may be a ring of gills around the posterior anus or the upper body surface; sides may bear tentaclelike cerata; torsion reversed in adults

Habits Marine, generally bottom dwellers; often in shallow coastal waters and on shores, especially among rocks and algae; sometimes in deeper water; a few are pelagic (live in open sea)

Breeding Hermaphrodites; mating occurs; eggs often laid in elaborate and conspicuous jellylike egg masses; larva emerges to develop in plankton before settling on appropriate substrate such as alga, shell, or rock

Diet Generally carnivorous; often specialists consuming one particular prey type or species

Habitat Widely distributed in most marine environments, especially coastal ones; some occur in oceanic planktonic habitats

Distribution All the world's seas and oceans

Sea lemon
(Archidoris
pseudoargus)

The great pond snail, *Lymnaea stagnalis*, is found in ponds and lakes throughout Europe and in the Baltic Sea. It is a scavenger and eats mostly plants, but also dead plant and animal matter.
Length about
2 inches (5 cm).

Common names Freshwater snails, terrestrial snails, terrestrial slugs

Subclass Pulmonata

Class Gastropoda

Phylum Mollusca

Number of species About 17,000

Size 0.04 in (1 mm) to 7 in (17 cm)

Great pond snail
(Lymnaea stagnalis)

Key features Lung formed from the mantle cavity; full torsion is usually reversed to some extent; shell present and body coiled, normally without operculum (freshwater and shore-dwelling snails); no shell and no obvious coiling (tropical slugs); shell present and body coiled (terrestrial snails) or reduced or absent, with body not obviously coiled (slugs); no operculum

Habits Aquatic (generally fresh water) and terrestrial; air breathing; terrestrial species found in damp or arid soils; often associated with vegetation and may hibernate in crevices in wood and stone; one group inhabits seashores and, like limpets, lives attached to rock surfaces

Breeding Hermaphrodites, but copulation, sometimes preceded by courtship, occurs; sperm transferred by special reproductive structures; eggs usually laid in egg masses on rocks, pond vegetation, or in soil; juveniles hatch from egg mass

Diet Herbivorous or carnivorous, using well-developed radula

Habitat Freshwater lakes, ponds, rivers, and associated vegetation; widely distributed in terrestrial environments; limited distribution in seashore environments

Distribution Subtropical and tropical seashores and on almost all landmasses worldwide

Oysters

Crassostrea virginica, the eastern oyster, is roughly pear shaped, but members of the species vary in size and shape. The outside of the shell is dirty gray or brownish in color, and the inside is white except for the muscle scar, which is deep purple. It is found in the Atlantic Ocean from the Gulf of St. Lawrence to the Gulf of Mexico and the West Indies. Length up to 8 inches (20 cm).

Eastern oyster
(Crassostrea virginica)

Common name
Oysters

Family Ostreidae

Order Ostreiformes

Class Bivalvia

Phylum Mollusca

Number of species About 40

Size Up to 8 in (20 cm), occasionally larger

Key features Adult body enclosed in 2 unequal shells, which move together by a hinge with reduced teeth; mantle opens all around the shell, and its left and right edges are not fused together; the inhalant and exhalant openings are weakly marked

Habits Nonburrowing marine bivalves generally living attached to hard surfaces such as other shells, rocks, and corals

Breeding Hermaphrodites—begin as male and change to female, then changing back to male again a number of times over seasons; sperm and eggs released into water via the exhalant water current, where external fertilization takes place; no courtship or mating behavior; planktonic larva results, which feeds in the plankton until settlement and metamorphosis; no maternal care

Diet Adults feed on suspended microorganisms and particles of detritus; free-swimming larvae feed on phytoplankton

Habitat Widely distributed in shallow marine environments, lagoons, estuaries, rocky shores, and reefs

Distribution Most of the world's seas and oceans except the polar regions

Nautiluses

The nautilus is the last of a vanishing line of cephalopods once abundant approximately 400 million years ago. *Nautilus pompilus* is known as the pearly nautilus. Shell diameter up to 10 inches (25 cm).

Pearly nautilus
(Nautilus pompilus)

Common name
Nautiluses

Order Tetrabranchia

Subclass Nautiloidea

Class Cephalopoda

Phylum Mollusca

Number of species About 6

Size Shell diameter up to about 10 in (25 cm)

Key features Conspicuous coiled, external shell divided into many chambers; outer surface of shell usually beautifully patterned, internal surface mother-of-pearl; adult body housed in the largest, newest chamber; older chambers help regulate buoyancy; head bears 80–90 suckerless tentacles protected by a hood; in males 4 tentacles are adapted to form the "mating arms" (the spadix); mantle cavity and siphon used in "jet propulsion"; mantle cavity contains 4 gills; eyes not as well developed as in squids and octopuses, and lack cornea and lens, functioning more like a pinhole camera; brain, statocyst, and nervous system also less well developed

Habits Adults are midwater predatory marine animals; found at various depths from shallow water down to 2,300 ft (700 m)

Breeding Sexes separate; mating achieved by the male transferring a packet of sperm into the female's mantle cavity using a group of modified arms; eggs laid on seabed; planktonic larval phase is present

Diet Carnivorous, relying on senses to detect mobile prey, which often includes crustaceans

Habitat Tropical seas from surface to midwater or near the bottom

Distribution Limited to certain parts of the southwestern Pacific Ocean

Cuttlefish and Squids

A *Loligo* species squid holds a captured fish in its jaw. *Loligo* paralyzes its prey with venom produced by its salivary glands. This squid is found in the warmer waters off the West Coast of North America. Length up to 8 inches (20 cm).

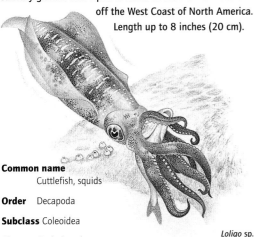

Loligo sp.

Common name
Cuttlefish, squids

Order Decapoda

Subclass Coleoidea

Class Cephalopoda

Phylum Mollusca

Number of species About 400

Size Length (excluding tentacles) from about 1.2 inches (3 cm) to 65 ft (20 m)

Key features Adult body short and flattened (cuttlefish) or long and torpedo shaped (squids), both with side fins; external shell lacking, but represented internally by a thick calcareous "cuttlebone" (cuttlefish) or a thin membranous horny "pen" (squid); 10 arms, 8 are similar in form, suckered, and shorter (1 modified in males for mating), 2 are longer; mantle cavity and siphon used in "jet propulsion"; cavity contains 2 gills; well-developed eyes with cornea and lens; brain and nervous system present; well-developed statocyst for balance and chromatophores for color change and camouflage

Habits Many adults are midwater- or surface-swimming predatory marine animals; some squids live in very deep water

Breeding Sexes separate; courtship and mating occur; male transfers sperm into female's mantle cavity using arm with specially modified suckers; planktonic larval phase is present

Diet Carnivores; well-developed hunting behavior using camouflage; prey subdued by toxic saliva injected using beaklike jaws

Habitat Most marine environments; more common in shallow coastal and pelagic (open) oceanic habitats

Distribution All the world's seas and oceans at all depths

Octopuses

Hapalochlaena lunulata, one of several species called the blue-ringed octopus, is found in the Indo-west Pacific and Indian Oceans. It is extremely toxic and can inflict a fatal bite. Arm span up to 8 inches (20 cm).

Pacific blue-ringed octopus (*Hapalochlaena lunulata*)

Common name
Octopuses

Order Octopoda

Subclass Coleoidea

Class Cephalopoda

Phylum Mollusca

Number of species About 200

Size Arm span from less than 2 in (5 cm) to 33 ft (10 m)

Key features Adult body usually round and relatively short; shell usually lacking, but occasionally present or may exist as a reduced internal structure; no lateral fins; 8 arms, all similar in form and linked by a web of skin for part of their length; suckers arranged in 1 or 2 rows; mantle cavity and siphon used in "jet propulsion"; mantle cavity contains 2 gills; well-developed eyes; brain and nervous system present; well-developed statocyst for balance and chromatophores for color change and camouflage

Habits Almost all adults are bottom-dwelling, predatory marine animals; many are solitary; behaviors complex, including use of ink to distract predators

Breeding Sexes separate; male transfers sperm into female's mantle cavity using arm with specially modified suckers; female often guards her eggs; planktonic larval phase present in many species

Diet Powerful carnivores; prey includes crustaceans, fish, and sometimes other octopuses; toxic saliva injected by well-developed beaklike jaws to subdue prey

Habitat Widely distributed in most marine environments, more common in shallow coastal habitats

Distribution All the world's seas and oceans

Sea Lilies and Feather Stars

Feather stars prefer to live above the seabed, often congregating on vertical rock faces and sometimes perching on other animals. The rosy feather star, *Antedon bifida*, is found in northwestern Europe. Size about 6 inches (15 cm).

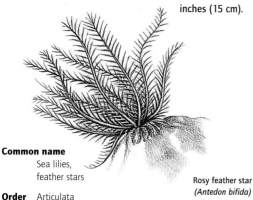

Rosy feather star
(*Antedon bifida*)

Common name Sea lilies, feather stars

Order Articulata

Class Crinoidea

Subphylum Crinozoa

Phylum Echinodermata

Number of species About 625

Size From 0.1 in (3 mm) to 3 ft (1 m)

Key features Adult body cup shaped; upper side bears featherlike arms in multiples of 5; underside of cup attached to substratum by flexible jointed stalk (sea lilies) or has jointed, clawlike cirri in groups of 5 (feather stars); color varied, often black, brown, or red; featherlike arms have side branches (pinnules); tube feet in clusters of 3 on arms and pinnules and in rows on either side of a food groove; head and brain absent

Habits Adults bottom-dwelling marine animals; sea lilies attached to hard base by a flexible stalk; feather stars free living but grip rocks and stones with cirri; sea lilies can swim for short periods by coordinated arm bending

Breeding No mating; sperm and eggs released into seawater; fertilization occurs outside the body; eggs hatch into microscopic planktonic larvae that metamorphose and settle on the substratum attached by a stalk; sea lilies retain stalk into adult life, feather stars break free from attachment as they develop

Diet Filter feeders, feeding on plankton and suspended organic particles

Habitat Exclusively marine, living on rocks, reefs, or deep-sea substratum

Distribution All the world's seas and oceans at all depths

Starfish, Brittle Stars, and Basket Stars

Ophiarachnella incrassata is a brittle star found on the Great Barrier Reef of Australia. Diameter 12 inches (30 cm). *Pisaster ochraceus* is found on rocky shores from Alaska to Baja California. Diameter 10 inches (25 cm).

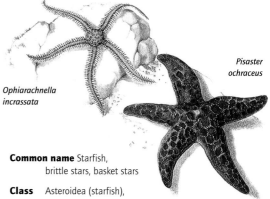

Pisaster ochraceus

Ophiarachnella incrassata

Common name Starfish, brittle stars, basket stars

Class Asteroidea (starfish), Ophiuroidea (brittle stars and basket stars)

Subphylum Asterozoa

Phylum Echinodermata

Number of species About 1,500 (Asteroidea); 2,000 (Ophiuroidea)

Size From 0.2 inches (4 mm) to 5 ft (1.5 m)

Key features Adult body star shaped; central body has 5 (occasionally more) arms; color varied, sometimes patterned; head and brain absent; no conspicuous sensory organs; flexible calcareous skeleton set in body wall; body surface covered in skin, sometimes decorated with spines; tube feet on underside of each arm, locomotion by tube feet (starfish) or arm movements (brittle stars and basket stars)

Habits Marine; adults live on seabed on rocks, reefs, and sand; normally lie with mouth against substratum; some burrow in sediments; movement in starfish generally by slow crawling using tube feet; brittle stars and basket stars move by flexing their arms

Breeding Courtship and mating absent; sexes usually separate; adults release sperm and eggs into seawater, where fertilization occurs; fertilized egg develops into microscopic larva that drifts in plankton; juveniles settle on seabed following metamorphosis

Diet Starfish are carnivores or detritus feeders; brittle stars feed on carrion, minute animals, detritus, or suspended food; basket stars are plankton and detritus feeders

Habitat Exclusively marine bottom dwellers

Distribution All the world's seas and oceans

Sea Urchins

Evechinus chloroticus is a regular (rounded) sea urchin with a mass of bristling spines and is found in rocky pools in New Zealand. Diameter 4 inches (10 cm). *Clypeaster rosaceus*, the brown sea biscuit, is very common around reefs in southern Florida, where it burrows just underneath the sand. Diameter 4.5 inches (11 cm).

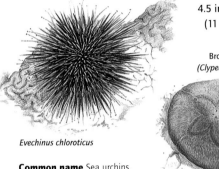

Brown sea biscuit
(*Clypeaster rosaceus*)

Evechinus chloroticus

Common name Sea urchins, sand dollars, heart urchins

Class Echinoidea

Subphylum Echinozoa

Phylum Echinodermata

Number of species About 950

Size 0.1 in (3 mm) to 7 in (17 cm)

Key features Adult body round, disklike, or heart shaped, showing 5-sided symmetry; colors varied, often black, green, gray, or brown; head and brain lacking; 5 paired rows of tube feet bearing suckers at tips; calcareous skeleton set in body wall (the test); test is usually rigid and bears mobile spines and minute grooming organs (pedicellariae) that may be venomous; many species have chewing organ (Aristotle's lantern) and teeth; long gut opens via mouth on underside and via anus on upper side of body

Habits Adults bottom-dwelling marine animals; usually lie with mouth downward; move using tube feet; spines used for defense and for burrowing in some forms

Breeding No mating behavior; sperm and eggs released into seawater; fertilization occurs outside the body; microscopic larvae generally planktonic; a few species brood their embryos

Diet Algae, sea grasses, encrusting invertebrate animals, and organic detritus

Habitat Exclusively marine, living on rocks and reefs or burrowing in sediment

Distribution All the world's seas and oceans at all depth

Sea Cucumbers

The sea cucumber *Pseudocolochirus axiologus* comes from the warm waters of the Pacific Ocean. Length 8–10 inches (20–25 cm).

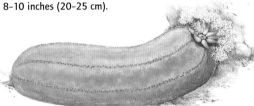

Common name Sea cucumbers

Pseudocolochirus axiologus

Class Holothuroidea

Subphylum Echinozoa

Phylum Echinodermata

Number of species About 1,150

Size 0.1 in (3 mm) to 5 ft (1.5 m)

Key features Adult body cylindrical or cucumber or sausage shaped, occasionally very elongated or slightly flattened; colors varied, often black or brown, sometimes patterned; 5-sided symmetry evident in the number of rows of tube feet on the body; no distinct head; anterior mouth surrounded by a ring of specialized, retractable, branched feeding tube feet (oral tentacles); no brain; tube feet used for moving usually bear suckers at tips; calcareous skeleton weakly developed, set in body wall, which is usually soft and flexible and lacks ornaments apart from warts; no jaws; long gut opens via anterior mouth and posterior anus

Habits Adults bottom-dwelling marine animals; animal lies on its side; locomotion by tube feet or wavelike contractions; some forms live in crevices or burrows

Breeding No mating; sperm and eggs released into seawater; fertilization occurs outside the body; eggs develop into microscopic planktonic larvae

Diet Detritus and plankton collected by deposit- or suspension-feeding oral tentacles

Habitat Exclusively marine, living on rocks and reefs or burrowing in sediment

Distribution All the world's seas and oceans at all depths

Glossary

Words in SMALL CAPITALS refer to other entries in the glossary.

Abdomen region of an ARTHROPOD's body behind the THORAX

Arthropod (PHYLUM Arthropoda) jointed-limbed invertebrate with hard-ended exoskeleton; includes insects, spiders, and crustaceans

Benthic living on or in the seabed

Bilateral symmetry symmetry in one plane, in which one side of an animal is an approximate mirror image of the other

Book lung in arachnids a paired chamber in the ventral wall in which the gaseous exchanges of respiration occur

Byssus threadlike filaments that attach some bivalves to rocks or plants

Carapace shield- or shell-like part of the exoskeleton; usually grows from the head

Cephalothorax combined head and THORAX, making up the front half of a spider's body

Cerci paired, articulated appendages at the end of the ABDOMEN; probably sensory

Chelicerae the pincerlike first appendages found in chelicerates

Cheliped THORACIC appendage with pincers, often very enlarged. *See* THORAX

Chitinous made of chitin, a protein that is an important component of many invertebrate bodies

Chromatophore cells in the skin of animals that can change color by contracting or expanding pigment

Cilium (pl. cilia) tiny hairlike projections growing from individual cells

Cirrus a slender, usually flexible appendage, e.g., an arm of a barnacle or a fused group of CILIA on some protozoans that functions as a limb

Clitellum the saddlelike region of earthworms that is prominent in sexually mature individuals

Cocoon silken case constructed by the LARVA in which the PUPA is formed

Commensal living in close association with another animal, not necessarily to its detriment

Cornicle small horn

Cremaster structure at the rearmost

tip of a PUPA, usually with tiny hooks to latch onto a silken pad spun by the caterpillar

Cyprid late LARVAL stage of barnacle

Cytostome cell mouth in HETEROTROPHIC single-celled animals

Elytron (pl. elytra) thickened leathery, often hard, front wing of most beetles

External fertilization fertilization in which egg and sperm are united outside the mother's body

Femur (pl. femurs, femora) third SEGMENT of an insect's leg

Flagellate single-celled animal that has one or more FLAGELLA

Flagellum (pl. flagella) whiplike structure growing from a single cell

Gamete reproductive cell (egg or sperm)

Gonads gland that produces GAMETES

Hair pencil cluster of hairlike scent scales usually tucked away within the body and protruded during courtship

Hermaphrodite has both male and female reproductive capability either simultaneously or as the result of a sex change

Heterotroph organism that takes its nutrients from consuming organic material derived from other organisms

Holoptic where the two eyes meet along the top of the head and almost touch

Instar the stage between molts of an ARTHROPOD

Internal fertilization fertilization in which the union of egg and sperm takes place inside the mother's body

Larva (pl. larvae) juvenile stage between egg and adult

Mandibles the first pair of mouthparts situated on the head

Mantle special region of the body wall, particularly of mollusks, that encloses the MANTLE CAVITY and may secrete the shell

Mantle cavity space enclosed by the MANTLE, through which water circulates, bringing oxygen and taking away waste products. Contains the gills and the reproductive and excretory openings

Maxillae the mouthparts immediately behind the MANDIBLES

Medusa free-swimming form of animals in the PHYLUM Cnidaria

Mesoglea middle layer of jellylike material between inner and outer layers of animals such as jellyfish and corals

Metamorphosis process of change by which one form develops into another, usually juvenile to adult

Nauplius early LARVAL stage of some crustaceans, usually free-swimming

Nymph the LARVA of an insect whose wings develop externally

Ocellus (pl. ocelli) simple eye

Ommatidium single unit of a compound eye; acts as a light receptor

Operculum buttonlike plate on the foot of gastropod mollusks, used to close the shell after the body has been withdrawn

Osmeterium scent gland found in the caterpillars of swallowtail butterflies

Ovipositor egg-laying structure

Palp SEGMENTED, fingerlike structure forming part of the mouthparts in insects, usually used for touch or taste

Papilla small protruberance

Parapodia SEGMENTAL appendages of some worms, usually covered in bristles

Parthenogenesis production of young by a female without mating with a male

Pectinate shaped like a comb

Pedipalp appendage (usually sensory) on the anterior part of the body of horseshoe crabs, scorpions, and spiders

Pelagic living in open water

Pheromone a chemical scent that produces a behavioral result in another animal, usually to attract or repel members of the opposite sex

Phylum a major group in the classification of animals, consisting of one or more classes

Phytoplankton microscopic algae suspended in surface water where there is sufficient light for photosynthesis

Plankton organisms, usually small to microscopic, that drift in the surface waters of rivers, lakes, and seas

Planula free-swimming early LARVAL stage of animals in the PHYLUM Cnidaria, including corals, anemones, and jellyfish

Pleopods paired abdominal appendages of certain aquatic crustaceans, usually adapted for swimming

Polyp SESSILE, tentacled form of animals in the PHYLUM Cnidaria

Predaceous describes an animal that preys on other animals for food

Proboscis tubelike feeding apparatus

Prolegs fleshy outgrowths in insect LARVAE that function as legs, but are not true articulated limbs

Pronotum protective shield covering the THORAX of an insect

Prothorax front SEGMENT of the THORAX

Pseudopod flowing foot or needlelike cell extensions used by amebas and other members of the PHYLUM Sarcodina for locomotion and feeding

Pupa (pl. pupae) the stage (usually static) between LARVA and adult insect in those with complete METAMORPHOSIS

Radial symmetry many-fold symmetry around a single central axis

IUCN CATEGORIES

EX Extinct, when there is no reasonable doubt that the last individual of the species has died.

EW Extinct in the Wild, when a species is known only to survive in captivity or as a naturalized population well outside the past range.

CR Critically Endangered, when a species is facing an extremely high risk of extinction in the wild in the immediate future.

EN Endangered, when a species is facing a very high risk of extinction in the wild in the near future.

VU Vulnerable, when a species is facing a high risk of extinction in the wild in the medium-term future.

LR Lower Risk, when a species has been evaluated and does not satisfy the criteria for CR, EN, or VU.

DD Data Deficient, when there is not enough information about a species to assess the risk of extinction.

NE Not Evaluated, species that have not been assessed by the IUCN criteria.

Further Reading   Index

Radula small, horny, tonguelike strip bearing teeth, used by many mollusks for scraping food

Rostrum piercing mouthparts of a bug; it consists of an outer sheath with two pairs of sharp STYLETS inside

Scutellum part of a bug's PRONOTUM that extends backward over the ABDOMEN; it is normally shield shaped

Sedentary permanently attached, nonmigratory

Segment a section of a body part

Sessile unable to move around

Siliceous containing silicate

Siphon tube leading in or out of the bodies of invertebrates (especially in mollusks) that is used to conduct water currents

Spermatophore packet of sperm produced by male and delivered to female during courtship or mating

Spinneret silk-producing apparatus

Statocyst balance organ

Stridulate generate sound by rubbing one part of the body against another

Stylets sharp mouthparts modified for piercing skin or the surface of plants

Symbiont organism living in mutually beneficial association with another

Tarsus (pl. tarsi) series of small SEGMENTS making up the last region of the leg of insects, the end bearing a pair of claws

Test external covering or "shell" of some invertebrates, especially sea urchins; lies just below the epidermis

Thorax (adj. thoracic) region of an insect's body behind the head; bears the legs and the wings (where present)

Tibia (pl. tibiae) fourth SEGMENT of an insect's leg, between the FEMUR and TARSUS

Vacuole a fluid-filled space within the cytoplasm (living matter) of a cell, bounded by a membrane

Zoea larva early LARVAL stage of crabs

Zooplankton small or minute animals that live freely in the water column

Barnes, R. D., *Invertebrate Zoology* (6th edn.), Saunders College Publishing, Philadelphia, PA, 1994.

Beer, A-J., et al. *World of Animals: Insects and Other Invertebrates* (Vols. 21–30), Grolier, Danbury, CT, 2004.

Campbell, A., and J. Dawes, *The New Encyclopedia of Aquatic Life*, Facts On File, New York, NY, 2004.

Meinkoth, N. A., *National Audubon Society Field Guide to North American Seashore Creatures*, Alfred A. Knopf, New York, NY, 1998.

Michener, C. D., *The Bees of the World*, Johns Hopkins University Press, Baltimore, MD, 2000.

Miller, S. S., *True Bugs: When Is a Bug Really a Bug?*, Franklin Watts Inc., New York, NY, 1998.

Milne, L., and M. Milne, *National Audubon Society Field Guide to North American Insects and Spiders*, Alfred A. Knopf, New York, NY, 1998.

O'Toole, C. (ed.), *The Encyclopedia of Insects*, Firefly Books, Toronto, Canada, 2002.

Preston-Mafham, K., and R. Preston-Mafham, *The Encyclopedia of Land Invertebrate Behavior*, MIT Press, Cambridge, MA, 1993.

Preston-Mafham, K., and R. Preston-Mafham, *The Natural History of Spiders*, Crowood Press, London, U.K., 1991.

Silsby, J. *Dragonflies of the World*, Smithsonian Institution Press, Washington, DC, 2001.

Useful Web Sites

http://animaldiversity.ummz.umich.edu/
University of Michigan Museum of Zoology animal diversity Web sites. Search for pictures and information about animals by class, family, and common name. Includes glossary.

http://www.arachnology.org
The International Society of Arachnology home page links to information on all sorts of arachnids.

http://earthlife.net/inverts
An amazing Web site full of information; includes obscure groups.

http://www.mnh.si.edu
Web site of the Smithsonian Museum of Natural History. Click on Museum Directory and then on Invertebrate Zoology for information about the museum's work on the study of invertebrate animals.

http://www.tolweb.org/tree
On more than 2,600 Web pages the Tree of Life provides information about the diversity of organisms on Earth, their history, and characteristics.